Saved Others Before Being Saved

*True stories of my life as a police officer
and then the day I was saved by God*

Jessie Frey

ISBN 978-1-64515-077-0 (paperback)
ISBN 978-1-64515-078-7 (digital)

Christian Faith Publishing, Inc.
832 Park Avenue
Meadville, PA 16335
www.christianfaithpublishing.com

Printed in the United States of America

Dedicated to all the men and women of law enforcement. Thank you for risking your lives to protect and serve others. God bless you!

Keep fighting the good fight.

CONTENTS

Prologue: Peacemaker 7

1. Rookie Year 11
2. Unthinkable Evil 20
3. New Police Department 28
4. Bloodbath 40
5. Evening Joy Ride 46
6. Victim or Suspect 50
7. Deranged Naked Guy 57
8. Unforgettable Ambulance Calls...63
9. Parents Not Parenting 74
10. Bar Fights..81
11. Robbery in Progress...89
12. Ugliness and Strangeness...93
13. Officer Needing Assistance...101
14. Three in the Afternoon 105
15. Troublesome Times 110
16. Deputy Sheriff for a Month..114
17. Led by Faith 122
18. Being Saved..127
19. Baptized 132
20. God's Timing 136

PROLOGUE: PEACEMAKER

Blessed are the peacemakers: for they shall be called the children of God.
—Matthew 5:9

Wearing the police badge for ten and a half years, from 2005 to 2015, was a rewarding experience where I got to be there for others in their time of need. Law enforcement not only requires that you risk your life to protect and serve others, but you also enforce state laws and city ordinances and be present to keep the peace through many difficult situations.

Remarkably prior to being hired as a patrolman, most officers don't realize that their main responsibility is being a peacemaker. Police officers respond to verbal or physical disturbances, domestics, and fights on a daily basis. As an officer, you have to take control of the scene, calm down all arguments, and listen to both sides of the conflict to see if there is a common ground.

A lot of times, there was no compromise between the individuals, so separation from each other would be suggested. Several times you would have to respond back to the address for the same individuals arguing or physically fighting. Unfortunately, some individuals never learned their lesson with verbal warnings and would need to be arrested for laws and city ordinances violated.

Law enforcement inspired me at a young age because I strongly wanted to help others and arrest anyone who had a crude, disrespectful personality (like my younger brother). In the state of Missouri, to be hired as a police officer, you had to be twenty-one years old, have a high school diploma or GED, no felony arrests, a thorough background and drug tests, and pass a POST Certification Class A license for law enforcement.

Growing up, it was only me, my younger brother, Anthony, and my mom. I had never met my biological father, and my brother's father left us when I was four years old. My mom did have a difficult time working and raising two children by herself, but she did her best for us. I remember when I was younger we had to use food stamps when it was the paper money, not on an EBT card like they have now. My mom personally disliked being on welfare and worked extra-long hours at her job to quickly get off it.

In the fourth grade, it started to become obvious to me that we did not have that much money. That was when Anthony, my brother, and I had to walk to elementary school on ice-covered roads. My mom had cut up pieces of carpet and glue them on the bottom of our tennis shoes. We still fell on the ice, but then we were laughing at the funny pieces of carpet on the bottom of our shoes.

As my brother Anthony grew up, he was continuously breaking the law. At the age of fifteen, he was stealing, smoking marijuana, drinking, taking other illegal drugs, prescription pills, always cussing and being disrespectful to our mother. It is precisely the reason to this day he is still being arrested by the same officers who worked with me.

My career as a police officer started on February 6, 2005, in the small town of Owensville, Missouri. The town had a population of 2,500 with only eight commissioned officers working for the police department. Approximately after a year and a half as a patrolman, I was promoted to corporal and I was also the school resource officer for the Owensville Police Department. Our department switched to a twelve-hour shift rotation, and I was scheduled to a permit shift of 3:00 p.m. to 3:00 am.

On November 3, 2008, I got hired as a patrolman at Rolla Police Department in Rolla, Missouri. The Rolla Police Department had thirty commissioned officers, and the town had a population of 19,000. Within the seven years of service as a police officer, I was promoted to senior patrol officer, traffic division officer, and assistant corporal.

All law enforcement, military personnel, first responders, firefighters, and paramedics need more respect and recognition for the jobs they do. They work long hours, responding to tough, stressful calls, usually never receiving a simple "thank you." Shockingly, most patrolmen do not make much over $13.00 an hour. I started at $9.50 an hour and took a decrease in pay to work for a larger police department in 2008 to receive more law enforcement experience.

As a police officer, I responded to many calls of distress. Those calls included domestics, assaults, physical fights, disturbances, robberies, property damages, vehicle accidents, fires, child abuse or neglect, animal cruelty, warrant of arrests, and deaths. Law enforcement officers are not only protecting all the citizens of the community, but we are also backup for other officers by shielding them, watching over them, and keeping them from harm. The Bible says in John 15:13: **"No one has greater love than this, that someone would lay down his life for his friends."**

Approximately two years after leaving law enforcement, I was questioning my purpose in life and asking God if I needed to get back into it. That's when God called me into fellowship with Him and the church and saved my life. The first time I went to church, at the age of thirty-four, I was saved by asking Jesus to come into my heart and be my Lord and Savior.

Then my life changed, and I became a new creation in Christ. I realized that God had been watching over me and protecting me my entire career as a patrolman. During this time, it also became obvious that everyone in law enforcement is really doing God's work by protecting His people, doing good deeds, and serving others.

This book contains true life events, personal experiences, and intriguing and risky calls that I responded to daily as a police officer over ten years. Only the names of the victims and suspects have been changed.

ROOKIE YEAR

Fresh out of the police academy on December 2004, I was ready to take on the world and fight the good fight to help save lives. Graduating with a State of Missouri Department of Public Safety Class A License from LETI (Law Enforcement Technical Institute) in Columbia, Missouri, I thought I knew what to expect.

It was February 6, 2005, when I got hired as a patrolman at the Owensville Police Department in Owensville, Missouri. Miraculously, the police department actually called me, asking if I was still interested in a police officer position. They informed me I would need to bring a completed application and résumé on the day of my interview. The police department informed that they received my name off a list of LETI Police Academy graduates. Immediately, I was shocked that an employer would contact me for a possible patrolman assignment. But then I had to locate the town in Missouri since I had never been there.

After passing all the background checks, interviews, drug screening tests, and being voted in by the city council members, I was then sworn into office as a police officer. My life changed overnight.

You observe events and individuals you never would have met outside of the law enforcement career. Most individuals are good, honest, polite, law-abiding citizens; but you have that small one percent. Those are the ones who lie, steal, destroy, do drugs, and kill. Police officers are introduced to the one percenter on a daily basis, and most of their calls for service are arresting individuals that broke the law.

Patrolling the streets, you have to handle so many different types of calls, but every task was new and challenging. The exciting part of the job was not knowing what the day had in store. You could have a slow day with only a few calls for service then the next minute you could have a multicar vehicle accident with several injuries or a death.

Officer's adrenaline would rise on high alert every time we heard the loud piercing tones set off on our portable handheld radios or patrol car radios. All law enforcement in Missouri learned that when they heard the high-pitched tones, it was an emergency call for immediate assistance. Our central communication 911 center dispatchers would sound the tones for robberies, domestic assaults, any home or vehicle fires, fights in progress, or vehicle accidents with injuries.

Responding to these emergency calls were referred to as a Code 3. Each patrolman was trained that while en route to a Code 3, they had to activate their patrol car's overhead lights and sirens and drive safely, quickly, and responsibly to their destinations. This meant yielding at intersections to make sure the coast was clear of oncoming traffic and cautiously passing motorists on the roadway. The last thing any officer wants to do is endanger themselves or another innocent person while heading to an emergency call to help others.

Working in law enforcement, you will be asked these top questions at least once during your career:

- "Do police officers have a quota for how many tickets they write or how many traffic stops they conduct a day?"
  No, police officers do not have a quota for how many tickets they write or traffic stops they produce on a shift. It has always been the officer's discretion to write a ticket, and I personally gave more verbal warnings than tickets.

- "Do all officers love donuts?"
  All the prior officers I worked with enjoyed and ate donuts. Truthfully, I would never eat donuts out in public while in uniform.

- "Is the police department open on weekends and on holidays?"
  Yes, and definitely if you need help, dial 911. Rookie officers quickly learn they work most weekends and holidays. Unfortunately for several years, new officers won't receive holidays off unless they requested them off using a vacation day.

- "Have you ever shot or Tasered anyone?"
  Personally, I never had to shoot anyone, but every officer knows that could be a possibility. In law enforcement, our job is to protect and serve the community so you might have to use deadly force to stop a suspect from harming or killing someone. I did Taser a male suspect with a knife in his hand. The suspect was safely arrested without any further injuries to himself or others.

On a daily basis, law enforcement arrest individuals for committing crimes and violating laws. Occasionally, officers will arrest the same individual more than once and certain suspects at least once every two weeks. These individuals were known as our regulars.

Police officers knew these individuals by name, where they lived, and what vehicles they owned. Consequently, no matter what you said to try to get these suspects or individuals to stop committing crimes or excessively drinking, they would not listen or obey the law.

On my first year as a patrolman, I met one of our town's regulars, a male in his early sixties named Larry, with shaggy gray hair and a stubbly gray beard. Every encounter with Larry was due to excessive drinking throughout the day.

One chilly morning in March, at approximately 8:00 a.m., I was dispatched to Larry's residence to check on him. The reporting party advised that they observed an older male lying outside on the grass near Larry's front porch.

Upon arrival, I noticed fresh frost covering the entire lawn. I parked my patrol car near the front of the residence. Walking toward the front door, I observed an older male lying facedown on the front lawn, a couple of feet from the small front porch. Approaching the male, I was able to identify him as the home owner Larry. He was wearing blue jeans and a short-sleeved tee shirt. I then noticed that Larry's dentures had popped out of his mouth and were lying on the ground near the right side of his head. Checking Larry's vitals, it was determined he was breathing and just sleeping.

As I woke Larry up, he mumbled in a slurred speech, "Leave me alone, I just want to go back to sleep." Turning my attention to Larry's dentures lying on the grass, I observed a huge plump slug crawling on his teeth. Oh my gosh, gross! Wearing latex gloves, I retrieved the dentures and continuously waved them back and forth until the slimy slug slowly oozed off.

Paramedics had arrived on the scene during this time and were checking over Larry's vitals. Further investigation revealed that Larry had consumed a lot of alcohol the prior night and had passed out in his front lawn sometime in the early morning. Larry was transported by ambulance to the hospital because he was unable to stay awake and answer simple questions.

Larry never would learn his lesson or stop drinking no matter how many times officers recommended it. Another unforgettable encounter with Larry was in June around three in the afternoon. Larry was wearing overalls with a white tee shirt, riding on a red lawn mower with a beer can in his right hand. Shockingly, Larry was riding the lawn mower undeniably slow on a busy highway, attempting to flag motorists to go around him.

Larry made a left turn onto a city street and pulled the riding lawn mower over to the side of the road. While speaking to Larry, his speech was slurred, he had glassy eyes, and he was unsteady on his feet. Larry just laughed when he was asked how much he had to drink. Larry said, "You know I drink too much." He did perform a few field sobriety tests, but failed them. Larry was placed under arrest for driving while intoxicated and transported to the police department.

Larry's riding lawn mower was placed on a flatbed wrecking truck and towed from the scene. Remarkably, this was my first time I observed a riding lawn mower being towed on a flatbed truck. It was a funny sight to witness. This had me thinking to myself, "Only in a small town."

Memorable Domestic Disturbance

It was six o'clock on a quiet Sunday morning, and I was the only officer on duty. Finishing up a report at the police station, I had exactly two hours until the next officer started his shift. Then I could head home for some much-needed sleep.

Suddenly, a loud high-pitched squeal sounded across my portable radio. Dispatch came across the radio, stating a domestic disturbance was occurring between a husband and wife in town.

I rushed out to my patrol car, as the dispatcher informed me that the Missouri State Highway patrol officer on duty was busy on another call and would not be responding to my location. This meant I would be the only officer responding to the domestic, and I had no one to call for help if I needed assistance.

Activating my overhead lights and sirens, I was en route to an unpredictable, possibly dangerous situation with no backup. Officers are trained that domestics can be one of the deadliest calls for law enforcement to respond to. People full of anger, rage, and hatred turn all those emotions toward the officer. Gathering all my inner strength and courage, I responded to the call.

Upon arrival, I was able to determine that both the husband and wife were intoxicated. The wife was screaming that her husband had thrown an open beer can at her, spraying her completely with beer. The husband admitted to throwing the beer at her because he said she would not be quiet and leave him alone. His wife yelled, "You need to arrest my husband now!"

I asked them if either one could leave the residence for a few hours to give each other some space. The wife said she had nowhere to go. Then her husband told me he was not leaving his residence unless I arrested him. I knew they needed to be separated and have time to become sober.

I placed the husband under arrest for a twelve-hour hold and informed him that as long as he was cooperative, no charges would be filed. I informed him they both just needed time apart to sober up. While I was walking him to my patrol car in handcuffs, his wife ran outside hysterically crying and demanding that I release him.

She was screaming that she loved him and that I should arrest her instead. The wife even attempted to grab her husband's arm and tried to pull him away from my grasp. I commanded her to get back or she would also be arrested with charges filed. His wife released her husband's arm but continued to wail uncontrollably, saying she would wait for him to get out of jail and she was so sorry. I was utterly shocked because I thought people only acted this bizarre on television. Never have I witnessed this behavior in real life. The husband shook his head and said, "Just take me to jail." I felt like an actor in a crazy movie scene. I was just waiting for someone to yell, "Cut!" It was absolutely that strange.

While placing him in my patrol car's caged backseat, he breathed a big sigh of relief and said, "Thank you." I looked in my rearview mirror as I pulled away from the residence, and the wife was still crying. Her husband appeared relieved to be getting away from the situation.

This was my first domestic disturbance, and I was the only officer on the scene. I believe I handled the situation to the best of my ability. I was able to calm down both individuals by separating them so they did not injure themselves or anyone else.

Check the Well-Being

On a peaceful Sunday morning in May, at approximately 6:30 a.m., I was dispatched to check the well-being of a male who appeared to be passed out in a vehicle parked in the middle of the street. Upon arrival, I located a white four-door passenger car parked in the middle of the road facing westbound. There was a loud engine revving sound coming from the parked car. Cautiously approaching the vehicle on the driver's side, I observed a male in his late fifties with gray hair sitting in the driver's seat with his head back, mouth slightly open and his eyes closed. I noticed that his right foot was pressing down on the gas pedal, causing the vehicle's engine to continue to rev. Miraculously, the male had placed the vehicle in park before he passed out. Otherwise, who knows what tragedies he could have caused himself or to others.

I tried to open the doors, but they were locked. Loudly, I began banging on the front driver-side window and yelling at the man to wake up. He slowly opened his eyes and appeared to be drowsy and lethargic.

In a commanding voice, I said, "This is the police department. Unlock your vehicle." The male just looked in my direction with a confused expression. Again, I said in a demanding voice, "This is the police. Open the door, or I have to open it for you."

A quick method police officers use to get into a secured vehicle is smashing out a passenger window. Rarely do I use force, but when an individual is not compliant to an officer's commands, I do. The male rolled down his window, and I could smell a strong odor of alcohol coming from the vehicle. I told him to turn off his vehicle and step out.

Argumentatively, the man kept saying he did nothing wrong and I had no reason to be harassing him since he had just pulled over to sleep for a moment.

As he slowly staggered out of the vehicle, I noticed that his eyes were bloodshot, and he smelled of alcohol. I informed him he had parked his car in the middle of the street with the engine still running, and his foot was pressing down on the gas pedal. I asked him how much he had to drink that night.

He said, "Only two beers."

Every law enforcement officer knows when an individual admits to drinking two beers; it is always double that amount. But for some reason, individuals will only say a "couple" or "two beers." The male continued to state he was okay to drive home and I had no reason to be bothering him.

I then had him perform a few field sobriety tests to verify if he could drive home. On the walk and turn test, he was unsteady on his feet, failed to walk in a straight line, and had to stop to steady himself on the turn. After he completed all the tests, it was apparent he was still intoxicated and should not be behind the wheel of a vehicle.

The male was placed in handcuffs and told he was under arrest for driving while intoxicated. Escorting him to my patrol car, I advised him I was glad that he was not involved in a vehicle accident and no one else was injured because of his careless act.

I transported him to the police department, but he was more agitated that I would not give him a ride home. Shaking my head, I thought some individuals never learn.

Warrant of Arrest

I arrived at a brick two-story residence at 8:30 p.m. in mid-August with another police officer. We were attempting to locate a seventeen-year-old named Trevor, with an active warrant for stealing. He was known to flee from the police.

We received information that Trevor was hiding out at his girlfriend's parents' two-story house located in town. An officer went to the front door as I walked toward the far-right rear corner of the house. At this location, I was able to observe the back door but still remained in earshot of the other officer. This was just in case our suspect attempted to run out the back door and I would be able to apprehend him.

A female, identified as the home owner, answered the front door. She was telling the officer that Trevor did not live there and she had no idea where he could be located. I heard the officer asking if he could do a quick walk-through to make sure Trevor had not gotten into her residence. The female continued to say Trevor was not there and refused to allow the officer into the residence. As I was standing outside near the back-right corner of the residence, I had to adjust my eyes to the darker backyard. Then I realized the streetlights were illuminating my shadow. Then I heard a shuffling noise coming from inside the residence on the second floor. The noise sounded like it was near the second-story rear window located above the back door.

As I pressed closer to the side of the residence, I hoped no one could see me or my shadow on the right side of the house. Suddenly, someone opened the rear window on the second floor. Then a young male with short brown hair, who was identified as Trevor, quickly stuck his entire head out the window. While leaning out the second-story window, Trevor looked at the ground then turned his head right and to the left to observe both sides of the house. Before I had time to contemplate what Trevor was thinking of doing, I observed him hang both of his feet over the window edge. He was going to jump.

Suddenly, the suspect leapt out of the window before I could react or yell not to jump. He landed on his bottom, miraculously, with no injuries. I removed my Taser from its holster and ran directly up behind the suspect, keeping it pointed at his back, ready to be deployed. I said, "Don't move or I will Taser you."

Without standing up, Trevor looked over his left shoulder and saw me. He hung his head down and placed both of his arms behind his back. I placed handcuffs on him and helped him to his feet. As Trevor stood up, I realized he was over six feet tall. Looking up at him, I said, "You are tall."

As I walked Trevor up to the front of the residence, I knew it had to be a sight to see. Here was a five-feet-four female officer escorting a slender over six feet tall seventeen-year-old male in hand-cuffs. I located the other officer still standing on the front porch with the home owner. I informed him that Trevor had jumped out of a rear window of the residence. Amazingly, the home owner actually became speechless when she observed me with Trevor. Undeniably, she knew she could be arrested and charged for hindering an investigation on a wanted suspect.

I would always remember this arrest as my "second-story jumper." Surprisingly, not all suspects try to get away from the police by jumping out of a window. I had no idea I would be arresting Trevor again in six years.

After one year of serving the community and patrolling the streets as a police officer, I could not wait to experience and observe what was next. I was aware it was going to continue being a mentally challenging career, but I was eager to help others and to keep learning and growing in law enforcement.

UNTHINKABLE EVIL

When you hear unthinkable evil, what type of situation or case do you think an officer would be experiencing?

For most individuals, the scenario that comes to mind is a murder scene or anything horrific with children.

Nothing prepared me for the unimaginable case I worked with only two years of experience in law enforcement under my belt. It truly was one of my hardest cases I had to investigate as a police officer.

It was March 16, 2007, a sunny Friday afternoon around 4:00 p.m., and I was reviewing a police report at the Owensville Police Department. I heard a loud knock on the booking room door. I opened the rear door and observed three females who said they needed to speak to an officer.

I contacted the central communications dispatcher by radio and informed them I was at the station taking a police report. The females were identified as a sixteen-year-old juvenile named Maia, who had straight blond hair just past her shoulders, wearing a white tank top and shorts. She was accompanied by her foster mom, identified as Cynthia, who was wearing a button-up blue blouse with khaki pants, and her biological mother, identified as Tammy. Tammy was wearing a spaghetti-strap gray tank top and short cutoff jean shorts with her long dark-brown hair pulled back in a messy ponytail. Maia's foster mother, Cynthia, stated they needed to file a police report for child endangerment.

I spoke alone with Cynthia in the main office area. She told me that Maia, her foster daughter, lives with her in Sullivan, Missouri, a town approximately thirty-five minutes away. Cynthia advised Maia's biological mother, Tammy, that she had recently been given court-ordered visitational rights to see Maia just this last summer. She informed me that Maia had been visiting her mother, Tammy, at her residence in Owensville since last summer and on a few weekends.

Just this past weekend, Cynthia said that Maia had pleaded with her to spend the night with a friend in Owensville, Missouri, and she allowed her to go. She informed me when she picked up Maia on Sunday evening, it was obvious Maia was not feeling good. She took her home and stated she gave her fluids to drink and made sure she got some rest while keeping an eye one her.

On Monday, Cynthia informed me that Maia did go to school, but then she received a call from Maia's principal advising that she needed to pick her up. Cynthia left work and went to Maia's high school. She was worried about Maia and stated why she needed to pick her up. Cynthia said Maia was a good student, with decent grades, who never had any disciplinary actions taken at school. Arriving at the high school, she entered the main office and contacted the principal and Maia. Cynthia said the principal told her Maia had involuntary movement, dilated pupils, a 120 pulse, and she needed to go to the hospital.

They went straight to the hospital, and Cynthia shockingly observed three small puncture marks on the inside of Maia's arm, indicating she had used a needle. Cynthia stated these were fresh unusual marks on Maia's arms she had never noticed before. While at the hospital, Cynthia said several blood tests were performed on Maia to determine what was in her system. Waiting a couple of hours, a doctor finally entered their room and told Cynthia and Maia the results of the blood tests.

Cynthia stated she was devastated to discover Maia had tested positive for methamphetamine and marijuana in her system. She mentioned she did ask Maia where she got the drugs because no drugs were allowed at their home. Cynthia said Maia told her she received the drugs from her biological father, Clint, who also resides in Owensville, Missouri. Surprisingly, Cynthia informed me that Maia had admitted to lying to her and confessed to spending the night at her father's apartment on Saturday night.

Cynthia intensely said that Maia had confided in her that while at Clint's apartment, he gave her some marijuana to smoke, and a needle was used to inject meth into her arm for the first time.

Cynthia was infuriated and said she wanted Clint arrested for giving Maia marijuana and meth and for placing her foster daughter's life in danger.

Next, I privately spoke to Maia's biological mother, Tammy, who informed me that this past summer in 2006, the courts had granted her visitations with her daughter, Maia. During this time, Tammy advised she also got reacquainted with Maia's biological father, Clint, after seeing him at a gas station in Owensville, Missouri. Tammy said Maia never got to meet her father, Clint, because when she was four years old, he was arrested.

Tammy informed me that her ex-husband Clint had been incarcerated in prison for the past twelve years and had recently been released. When she ran into Clint, she had asked him if he wanted to meet his daughter. He did agree to it.

In June of 2006, Tammy stated she introduced Maia to Clint at his apartment in Owensville, Missouri. She informed me that Maia had frequently visited her and Clint several times throughout the summer.

Tammy informed me she just found out today that Clint had given Maia marijuana and meth. She admitted to swinging by Clint's apartment prior to arriving at the police department today. Tammy said she had screamed in Clint's face, yelling that she was reporting him to the police and told him he was going back to jail. Tammy stated she wanted Maia's biological father, Clint, arrested right now for giving her daughter drugs.

I followed Tammy back into the police department booking room where Cynthia and Maia were waiting. I assured them that evidence would be gathered to give to the Prosecuting Attorney's Office so that warrants and an arrest could be made. They were all given a strong warning not to have any further contact with Clint.

Afterward, when all three individuals left the police station, I mentioned the current child endangerment case to the chief of police and several other officers. It was decided to do a knock and talk at the suspect's apartment in Owensville.

Arriving at a ·small brown brick one-bedroom apartment at approximately 5:30 p.m., I knocked on the front door while another officer walked toward the back of the apartment duplex. With no answer, I continued to knock loudly on the front door. Finally, a male, thirty-six years old, five feet nine tall, with short brown spiky hair and a goatee, who was identified as Clint, answered the front door. Clint said he was asleep on the couch and did not hear us knocking on his front door.

I Informed Clint that I was aware his ex-wife, Tammy, had contacted him about his daughter, Maia, going to school with drugs in her system. Clint stated that Tammy did arrive at his apartment early that afternoon and was screaming at him something about giving her daughter drugs. He said that was not true and we were welcome to search his residence for drugs.

A walk-through of his residence with two other officers was conducted. When a walk-through is performed, officers are looking for illegal or suspicious items involved in a crime, located in plain view on top of tables, counters, or bookshelves. It is a brisk search unless the suspect gives permission to open drawers or cabinets to go through.

Speaking to Clint, I asked him if he had smoked anything besides cigarettes or tobacco in his apartment. Clint admitted to smoking a joint every now and then but refused to smoke when his daughter was in his apartment. No illegal narcotics or drug paraphernalia was located.

Two days later, I received a disturbing phone call while on shift at the police department from Maia's biological mother, Tammy. Tammy frantically told me that Maia had just confessed to her that she had been having sex with her biological father, Clint.

This started just two months after she reconnected with him this past summer. Tammy stated that Maia said Clint had told her not to tell anyone because he would go back to prison for a long time.

Immediately, I informed Tammy that an interview would need to be conducted at the Children's Advocacy Center. It would be scheduled with a Children's forensic interviewer, Maia, and Cynthia, her foster mother, since Maia was sixteen years old.

The interview occurred a couple of days later in Sullivan, Missouri. I witnessed the interview in the next room on security cameras, as it was being recorded for the Prosecuting Attorney's Office as evidence.

Maia stated to the forensic interviewer she had just recently met her biological father, Clint, in the summer of 2006 because he had been in prison for twelve years. She said her biological mother, Tammy, had taken her over to her dad's apartment and she had spent the weekend with him. Maia said her dad would flirt with her and tell her "if you weren't mine."

She thought the first time they had intercourse was around a month and a half after they met. Maia said the last time she was at her father's apartment was either two or three weekends ago. Maia said she was looking at a magazine, and her father asked if she wanted some meth. She said she told him, "I guess."

Maia stated her father shot her up in the arm with a needle, but the first hit of meth had too much water in it so Clint shot her up again with another syringe. She informed us afterward she had a major headache and couldn't breathe so she opened his refrigerator door and stuck her head in, just to help her catch her breath.

Maia told the investigator that after the meth, they both smoked a joint that contained marijuana. She said her father then took off all her clothes and they had sex. Maia said Clint would brainwash her and tell her how he didn't think she was his daughter. He had told her not to tell anyone because he would get a long time in jail.

After the interview and collecting all the evidence, warrants were issued through the Prosecuting Attorney's Office for Clint's arrest. Several attempts were made to locate Clint at his apartment so an arrest could be made, but officers were unable to locate him.

Surprisingly, Clint heard the police were attempting to locate him, and he had the audacity to call the Owensville Police Department to ask why the cops were looking for him. Answering the call, I informed Clint there was an active investigation against him and he needed to come to the police station.

Desperately, Clint continued to ask me if he was going to be arrested. I knew if he knew there were warrants for his arrest, he would flee so I advised it was an active investigation. Clint informed me he was at work now but would arrive at the department this afternoon to clear his name. Clint said he would not run from the police because he was still on probation for five years.

Coincidentally, Clint failed to arrive at the police department that afternoon. Officers kept surveillance on his residence in case he returned home to retrieve items, but he did not return home.

A couple of days later, without a trace of Clint, I received another phone call at the police station from Tammy, Maia's mother. Tammy urgently informed me Maia had mentioned that when Clint was running from the police in the past, he would retreat to a friend named Ed. His home was located in another small town. She gave me a description of a white house at the end of a county road with a beat-up maroon pickup truck. Tammy said Maia did not know Ed's address, but knew the directions to the residence.

I passed on all the information to a county sheriff deputy and also informed them that the male suspect, Clint, had an active warrant for his arrest. Amazingly, that day, deputies located Clint concealing himself in a rear bedroom inside his friend Ed's residence. He was taken into custody without incident.

On April 6, 2007, deputies transported Clint to the Owensville Police Department. He arrived at the police station at noon, and I read him his Miranda rights before the interview began. Clint stated he understood his rights and was willing to talk to me.

He stated he had recently seen his ex-wife, Tammy, over the summer of 2006 at a gas station and she told him his daughter, Maia, wanted to meet him. Clint said he had not seen his daughter since she was a baby so he agreed to meet her. Clint informed me Tammy brought Maia over to his apartment for the first time around June and then Maia would occasionally visit him on weekends by herself.

I inquired about Maia's behavior and actions around him. Clint said that the clothing Maia wore, the skintight shirts and skimpy shorts, and her behavior around him made him think she was wanting to have sex with him. Clint said Maia became flirtier toward him, and he noticed the way she would look at him. This was when Clint said that he realized Maia had become infatuated with him. He said that Maia would always talk about sex around him, and he honestly believed it was to make him jealous.

While interviewing Clint, he continued to deny any wrongdoing and attempted to place the entire blame on his daughter, Maia. Clint persistently stated it was the clothing Maia wore and her flirty actions around him that made him think she wanted him.

Clint was informed of all the felony charges filed against him. They were statutory rape in the second degree, endangering the welfare of a child in the first degree, and incest. Afterward, officers transported Clint to the county jail where he was incarcerated until his trial.

Four years later in May of 2011, I had a subpoena to appear in court to testify in front of a judge and jury about the case. The suspect, Clint, was still locked up in the county jail and was transported to the courthouse by correctional officers. Later, I was informed by a correctional officer that Clint had apparently decided to smuggle marijuana on him into the courthouse. Needless to say, more charges were added to his sentence.

Before the trial began, while waiting in the hallway outside of the courtroom, I was approached by two females who were identified as Maia and her biological mother, Tammy. Maia was now twenty years old, married with her own family and expecting her second child.

Graciously, Tammy thanked me for all the work I had done on the investigation and getting charges filed against Clint. She stated she was pleased to see that her ex-husband Clint was still in jail for the crimes he had committed against her daughter.

At the completion of the trial, I was informed the jury found Clint guilty of all the charges. The judge sentenced Clint to twenty years in prison, and he was transported back to the county jail by the correctional officers. I was glad to see justice prevail over evil.

As a law enforcement officer, we see evil on a daily basis, just disguised with many faces. We continue to fight the good fight doing God's work He has called us to do, whether we realize it at the time or not until a few years later.

New Police Department

Being a police officer of the city of Owensville for the past three and a half years was an honorable and great learning experience. But I felt compelled to move to a larger police department to receive more responsibilities, help more people, and answer more calls for service.

I was excited to see what adventures were next in my life as I applied to the Rolla Police Department. Prior to starting the new job, a hiring process had to be completed. An application, résumé, background checks, drug tests, a written psychological test, and a polygraph test were required.

I had never performed a polygraph test (also known as lie detector test) before this, so I was not sure what to expect. Anxiously arriving at the police department, I was escorted by a lieutenant to a tiny interview room with one door and no windows. While being hooked up to the machine, a wire was placed above my chest and then a finger clamp, or a pulse oximeter, was clipped on my index finger. The instrument used during a polygraph test receives and records changes in a person's pulse and breathing rates. Before the test began, the lieutenant informed me to answer every question truthfully with a yes or no response only. Nervously, I informed him I understood, and the test began.

Consequently, while being interviewed, I could feel my heart beating in my chest. I tried to slow down my heart rate and pulse by breathing slower, but I could still feel the strong thumping sensation in my finger. Remarkably, my nervousness and anxiousness did not alter the test results and I passed. Next on the schedule was an interview in front of three of the police department staff.

On November 03, 2008, I was sworn in as a patrolman at the Rolla Police Department in Rolla, Missouri. Now I was a police officer for a larger department with thirty certified officers and in a town with a population of 19,000. I also met my future husband, David, who was a sergeant with the department. At the time, it was unbeknownst to me that two years later we would end up dating. But things have a way of working themselves out for God's purpose and plans.

While working for the Rolla Police Department, I responded to emergency calls and calls for service daily. Every officer call and traffic stop required documentation or a police report. Trust me, report writing is the part of the job most officers never enjoy, but know it has to be done. Personally, I did not like to write traffic summonses. I gave more verbal warnings to polite, cooperative individuals on traffic stops. But as an officer, you are required to enforce the law and keep everyone safe.

As a law enforcement officer, you are always running toward danger or uncertainties while other individuals are running away. Technically, my favorite part of being a police officer was accelerating to high-risk calls where crimes were in progress or individuals needed immediate help.

Responding to an emergency call with my patrol car's lights and sirens activated, it was not uncommon to pass another patrol car traveling in the opposite direction going to a separate disturbance. We waved as we passed, but continued in opposite directions to our set emergencies. Those were busy, but exciting times.

All patrolmen have had individuals attempt to hide or conceal themselves from detection or custody. Suspects usually hide out for only one reason: they do not want to be arrested or go back to jail. It was always comical when discovering a person concealing himself from view because you automatically knew that individual probably had a warrant or had committed a serious crime.

Suspects Trying to Hide

Arriving at a small two-story apartment, I attempted to serve a search warrant on a twenty-year-old male for stealing. Unable to locate the suspect in any of the downstairs rooms, I made my way upstairs. The first bedroom on the right at the top of the stairs appeared to be the main bedroom. As I entered the room, it was a complete mess. Clothing was tossed everywhere and covered the floor. The bedspread was lying halfway on the bed and the floor, and several dresser drawers were half pulled out with clothes peeking over the edges. The closet door was completely closed. Cautiously opening the closet door, I viewed a ghostly shaped human figure sitting on the floor with a light-blue blanket hanging over him. I laughed to myself because the person underneath the blanket believed he was invisible with the blanket covering over him.

I commanded the individual to come out from underneath the blanket; he remained still like a covered statue. Shaking my head, I told the individual I had seen him and to come out of the closet. Surprisingly, an older female in her midforties crawled out from underneath the blue blanket. I thought it would be the male suspect I was expecting to locate at the apartment. I ran the female's information through our central communications 911 Center and was advised that the female had an active warrant for failure to appear on an original charge for stealing.

At first, she tried to deny having any charge against her because she said she had shown up at court for the stealing charge. She said she was not sure why she tried to hide in the closet from the police. I placed her under arrest for her active warrant and escorted her outside to my patrol car.

Burglary Suspect

One late evening, we attempted to serve a search warrant on a twenty-seven-year-old black male who had an active warrant on an original charge of burglary and possession of drugs. We received information from a witness who told us they observed the suspect hiding out at his mother's residence. When we arrived at the residence, his mother said her son had been there but had left a few days earlier. She said she had no idea where he was headed, only that he had said he would not be returning back home.

We asked to do a quick search of the residence to verify that he was not there and she agreed. We were unable to locate the suspect on the main floor, so we went upstairs. We entered a large bedroom and saw a seventeen-year-old female sitting on the bed. She had an alarmed expression on her face. When we asked her why she was not downstairs with the rest of her family, she would not answer right away. The girl finally said she was unaware the police were in their home and she was the only one in her room. One of the officers escorted her back downstairs to the other family members waiting in the living room until the search was finished.

We were unable to locate anyone else in the bedroom. I observed a large framed square on the wall on the opposite side of the bed. It resembled a small storage door without a handle that took up only half of the wall. I remembered our house when I was growing up, and it had a small storage door that led to a little crawl space, which was great for hiding. I pulled on the square, and it popped right off the wall. I handed it to the officer next to me. Inside was a small attic-type crawl space with insulation on the floor. I pulled my Taser out of its holster and aimed it inside the space. The other three officers next to me had their guns out of their holsters too in case the suspect was hiding inside with a gun or any other weapon.

On the left side, I noticed a wall. To the right side, I observed only the lower half of an individual. It was hard to believe that our suspect was sitting on the floor resting against the right-side wall. His left hand was on the ground, but I was unable to see his right hand. I commanded him to come out of the cramped space, but he just sat there.

I told him I could see his hand. Amusingly, he tried to prevent me from seeing his hand by curling it behind his back. Again, I commanded him to exit the crawl space now or he was going to be Tased.

The male began to slowly crawl toward the opening in the wall. When he got to the entrance, he was ordered to lie down on the ground. He failed to comply, so we assisted him to the ground and applied handcuffs. After searching him and verifying he did not have any weapons, he was escorted downstairs.

The suspect's mother and sister were told how there could have been charges filed against them for hindering the investigation.

Fast Runner

One afternoon, I responded to a residence for a twenty-two-year-old black male named Aaron, who had an active warrant for possession of drugs and distributing.

Aaron's girlfriend, Zoey, had called the police department earlier in the morning trying to get him arrested for stealing their vehicle, which was registered in both their names. I informed her that no crime had occurred if both of their names were on the vehicle's registration, and she could not file charges for a stolen vehicle. Zoey stated that her boyfriend, Aaron, did have an active warrant for his arrest. I told her if that were true, when I ran his information, he could be arrested for the warrant. Zoey was advised to call us when Aaron returned to the residence and we would contact him.

Three hours later, Zoey called the police department again to tell us Aaron had just arrived home with their vehicle. As I arrived at the scene, I parked a block from the residence. Before I approached the front porch, Zoey opened the front door. She yelled, "Aaron just took off running out the back door." Zoey said she was furious at Aaron for taking her car so she told him the cops were there to arrest him.

I ran toward the backyard and recognized the suspect as he turned to look back over his right shoulder. With an alarmed expression on his face, he quickly looked away, leaped over a wire fence, and continued running toward the street. Other officers en route to my location were informed the suspect was observed running northbound on Leroy Street. He then veered to the right, cutting between several houses.

I attempted to locate the suspect as he was running up a hill. Thankfully, I heard a dog in the area barking continuously. The dog was barking through a wooden fence toward an older detached metal shed. Another officer arrived at my location and assisted in searching the shed. The suspect was located hiding in the shed and placed in handcuffs.

When I ran Aaron's information through central communications, I was informed he did have an active warrant for distribution and possession of drugs. After patting him down for any weapons or drugs, Aaron was transported to the county jail. While at the jail, we ask all suspects if they have any drugs concealed on them and to let us know before they enter the correction facility. Otherwise, it would be another felony charge added to their charges.

Aaron denied having any narcotics on him. The jailers started collecting all his personal belongings to document and secure them. A jailer had Aaron take off his tennis shoes, and underneath the inside memory foam was a small plastic baggie containing a white powdery substance. First thing out of Aaron's mouth was, "Those are not my shoes."

Occasionally, I have heard a suspect say those are not my pants when marijuana was located in the front jeans pocket; but never "those are not my shoes." I laughed to myself because technically, the tennis shoes were his size and he could run perfectly well in them.

Aaron said, "I don't know what that white powder is in the shoes."

He said if he realized the small baggie with white powder was in the shoes, he would have disposed of it before the police found him.

We tested the white powder residue while at the jail. It tested positive for heroin. Aaron put his head down and refused to make eye contact. He was informed a charge for possession of heroin would be added to his other charges.

Hiding in Plain View

Most of our suspects lie to police officers on a daily basis, so it makes it difficult to take what they tell us as the full truth. For instance, if an individual does not know their social security number by the age twenty, that is a huge red flag they may be hiding their identity because they could have warrants.

On a Friday night around 10:30 p.m., I was patrolling near the movie theater on Forum Drive. Traveling directly in front of me was a black four-door vehicle with its rear passenger side taillight not operating. I activated my overhead lights and sirens, and the vehicle made a quick right turn into a vacant parking lot. After I radioed in to dispatch my location and the vehicle registration to dispatch, I approached the driver on the driver's side of the vehicle.

The driver was a male in his early thirties who stated he was from Kansas City, Missouri, but he did not have his driver's license on him. He knew his social security number. So I gathered his information and passed it on to central communications to run the individual's driving status through Missouri. He came back not on file.

Dispatch advised me that the date of birth was wrong. The correct date of birth with that name and social was off by a couple of days. I thought this was odd. So I walked back up to the driver and asked him to verify all his information again. He confirmed all same information with the same wrong date of birth.

During this time, the police sergeant had pulled up behind my patrol car, and I informed him of the situation. A DMV (Department of Motor Vehicles) picture of the individual with the name and social security number he continued to give was sent to me from our central communications 911 Center. My driver had several features matching this individual, but the male pictured visibly weighed more than my driver and had no tattoos listed. My suspect had several tattoos on his arms.

It was decided that the suspect be taken back to the police department to send his fingerprints off to verify who he really was. The suspect was informed his information was not on file so to completely identify him, we were going to collect his fingerprints. The male was placed in handcuffs and detained until we could identify who he was and that he had a valid license.

While at the station, the male was placed in a temporary holding cell after being fingerprinted to await his results. Within thirty minutes, he was identified as a wanted felon out of Kansas City,

Missouri. Shockingly, he was number ten on the Kansas City top ten most wanted list. Further investigation revealed that the information he continued to give me was his brother's information. Oddly enough, he could not remember his brother's correct date of birth, which got him caught.

Even the suspect was surprised we caught him because he had been running from the police for months. He stated he had been using his older brother's pedigree information the entire time without being discovered. It was just another day at work attempting to locate suspects who consider it all right to run and hide without being accountable for the crimes they have committed. With every passing year in law enforcement, you will observe suspects performing wilder incidents to keep from being arrested.

St. Patrick's Week

In Rolla, Missouri, St. Patrick's week was the busiest week for all the city officers. Before the week even begins, all patrolmen prepare themselves for a week of disturbances, fights, checking on intoxicated people, destruction of property, and sexual assaults. Service officers enjoyed this week because they were guaranteed to physically detain intoxicated individuals from harming themselves or others or stop fights while in progress.

For the entire week, during the day, it was not uncommon to observe college students outside on the front lawn of their fraternity houses, lounging on couches and drinking beer. During St. Patrick's week, students would drink, play beer pong, and party nonstop.

At the end of the week on Saturday night, dispatch would send officers to check the well-being of intoxicated individuals who were staggering near the road. When I responded to one of the calls, I observed seven individuals stumbling in separate directions, all wearing green sweatshirts. It was apparent they had been drinking that night. In this situation, you scan the area for the most intoxicated individual to check on.

For the St. Patrick's Day parade, college students were literally allowed to paint Pine Street, a main street located downtown, green. Parade detail was police officers who had to handle crowd and traffic control. This was not a relaxing gig. There was a minimum of five rows of people all pushing forward past the marked lines to grab candy or novelties. After directing one-half of the intersection to take several steps back toward the marked line, the other half moved forward past the line again. Plus, during the St. Patrick's Day parade, individuals aged twenty-one or older were allowed to drink and carry open containers of alcohol.

On a Wednesday afternoon, at approximately 5:00 p.m., the start of St. Patrick's week, I was patrolling the downtown area on Pine Street near a local bar. The moment I drove past the bar, I observed a male, later identified as Travis, in his early twenties, with a brown medium-length mohawk, wearing a white tee shirt and blue jeans, burst through the bar door and take off running in a sprint. Suddenly, an officer shoved the bar door open and ran after him.

Without hesitation, I threw my patrol car in park, locked the doors, and raced after the officer and suspect. Across my portable radio, I heard the officer call out how he was in foot pursuit with the suspect. I radioed in to dispatch that I was following behind the officer. Travis made a quick left turn, sprinting toward the rear of the building where the railroad tracks were located.

Travis was so intoxicated he ended up stumbling on the gravel rocks located directly behind the bar, falling face-first onto the ground near railroad tracks. The primary officer was able to get on top of the suspect and was holding him down prior to my arrival. Travis was angry, cursing, and screaming the entire time, "You beeping pigs!" He also continued to fight the officer and got to his feet. To prevent Travis from fighting anymore, the officer had hosed his face with pepper spray. Needless to say, Travis had an orange mohawk by the end of the ordeal.

I assisted the officer in handcuffing Travis and keeping him down on the ground. During this time, another officer arrived on the scene and assisted so Travis would not punch any of us.

Travis yelled, "Oh, you think you're so tough? But it took five of you to hold me down."

I informed him, "No, only three officers held you down, and I was one of them."

Surprisingly, the intoxicated suspect did apologize, but as I was walking him to the patrol car, he observed people standing outside the bar watching the scenario.

So Travis yelled, "These beeping pigs!"

I placed him in the backseat of the patrol car and closed the door. This was only day one of an entertaining St. Patrick's week.

Four-Wheeler Arrest

Then on Friday evening during St. Patrick's week, at approximately eight thirty, as I was patrolling around several fraternity houses, I observed several college students congregating on their front lawns with open beer bottles.

Dispatch then put out a broadcast of an individual operating a four-wheeler on Kings Highway, a congested road with a lot of local fast-food restaurants. I turned onto Tenth Street and came to a complete stop at a red light. I was waiting to make a left turn onto Highway 63. After I made a left turn on Highway 63, I would then make a right at the next intersection, which was Kings Highway. I would then cruise the area to attempt to locate the individual operating an ATV on the highway. Honestly, I believed the suspect had already fled the area and there would be no way of locating him.

Imagine my surprise when suddenly I observed a four-wheeler being operated by a male in his early twenties with another male sitting behind him. The ATV accelerated past me, traveling north-bound on Highway 63. I just shook my head in disbelief.

I quickly made a right turn onto Highway 63 and pulled directly behind the ATV. I activated my lights and siren and attempted to initiate a traffic stop on the four-wheeler. The male operator turned his head to look over his right shoulder and saw me directly behind him. Instead of slowing down or finding a location to safely pull over, the suspect rolled on the throttle and leaned forward. The four-wheeler lunged forward and begin to accelerate. The male passenger frantically started waving his arms and appeared to be yelling at the operator either to stop or slow down.

Shockingly, the operator made a quick right turn onto a city street from the highway. Horrifically as the ATV turned the corner, I observed both the front and rear tires on the right side raise several inches off the road. The rear seat passenger was still waving his arms and had to grab ahold of his seat so he wouldn't be thrown off.

I slowed down and gave the suspect some distance, just in case he lost control, wrecked, or lost his passenger. The last thing I wanted to do was cause the driver to have a careless accident.

Thankfully, the four-wheeler got back on all four tires and accelerated up the city street. I radioed to the other officers, informing them of my location and that I was in pursuit of the ATV. It was failing to stop for me. The operator raced up the windy road to a stop sign. Outraged, I could not believe how the operator was putting himself, the life of his passenger, and anyone else on the road in possible danger.

As I approached the stop sign, I was waiting for the suspect to make another quick turn and to keep accelerating. Shockingly, the operator slowed to a stop. Exiting my patrol car with my gun in my right hand, I ordered the suspect to turn off the vehicle. The passenger had both his arms raised up in the air above his head before I even exited my vehicle.

The driver got off the four-wheeler. The suspect, Benjamin, was a twenty-one-year-old, with short brown hair, six feet two, and over two hundred pounds. Benjamin kept repeating in a slurred speech that he "was sorry." A strong odor of alcohol was emitting from his breath. I asked him how much he had to drink. He hung his head down and said, "A couple of beers."

I placed Benjamin under arrest for operating the four-wheeler on a public highway while intoxicated. After handcuffing Benjamin, I walked him over to my patrol car and put him in the backseat. Benjamin complained the entire time about how he could not fit. I informed him it was a temporary ride to the jail.

I then approached the frightened passenger, Alan, who was still sitting on the four-wheeler with his arms raised. Alan asked, "Can I put my arms down now?" Trying not to laugh, I advised him he could. I had him sit on the curb along the side of the road and wait until someone picked him up. Sincerely, Alan said he was trying to get his friend, Benjamin, to stop the four-wheeler and pull over when he saw the cop car behind them. He said to me that Benjamin would not slow down and even decided to speed up.

I told Alan I was relieved neither of them was injured during Benjamin's reckless driving. Intensely nodding his head, Alan agreed and apologized for his friend's actions.

Unbelievably, many individuals celebrate St. Patrick's Day by consuming alcohol for the entire week. It makes for a long, but entertaining week because officers have to handle call after call pertaining to one or more intoxicated individuals. Our job as a patrolman is to protect individuals from themselves or from others if needed, and that is exactly what we do with all our strength and courage.

BLOODBATH

It was an extremely cold January morning at two o'clock when I was patrolling the snow-covered streets. My patrol car was making fresh tire tracks in the snow, and it was apparent no traffic had been on the streets for a while. Looking around, there were no fresh footprints on the sidewalks or streets, indicating that everyone must be in their warm houses for the night. I decided to drive back to the police station to finish up some paperwork, when a loud piercing alarm went off on my patrol car radio, breaking the silence.

Dispatch was informing another patrolman of a disturbance call in progress. The dispatcher stated that an unknown female was heard from outside the caller's residence near the 200 Block of Olive Street in Rolla, Missouri, screaming for help.

We were told the female was observed standing next to a silver four-door passenger car parked directly in front of the reporting party's residence. Dispatch stated the female was described to be in her early twenties with shoulder-length brown hair, wearing a white shirt with dark-blue winter jacket and blue jeans.

Dispatch then got back on the radio, advising that a male suspect was observed standing in front of the female and who appeared to be shoving her into the silver passenger car. The male was described as a white male with short blond hair in his early twenties wearing a white tank top and blue jeans.

Realizing I was only five blocks away from the caller's residence, I activated my overhead lights and sirens and responded quickly to the location. I turned a corner a tad too fast, and the rear of my patrol car skidded to left and then to the right, reminding me to slow down due to the snow on the roads. I knew I would not be able to help anyone if I injured myself or got into an accident while responding to the disturbance.

I made a right turn onto Holloway Street and was traveling northbound down a slight hill. I turned off my sirens and lights prior to reaching the location so I would not announce my presence to the suspect. Suddenly, I realized I had accidentally passed the street where the suspect's vehicle was parked. I slammed on my brakes so I could stop, but my patrol car continued to slide forward on Holloway Street. I looked for a street I could use to rapidly turn around, and the alarm alerted again on the patrol car radio.

Dispatch announced across the air that the suspect involved in the disturbance was leaving the area driving the silver passenger car. We were informed the caller was not able to see the female inside the vehicle but believed she was inside the car. Before I could react, our dispatcher then stated that the suspect's vehicle had just made a left turn onto Holloway Street, traveling northbound.

As I glanced into my rearview mirror, I observed the silver car traveling down the slight hill directly behind me. I was astonished to see the suspect traveling in my direction. I thought to myself, "What are the odds of that happening?"

Without even thinking about it, I slammed my patrol car in park while stopping in the middle of road and threw on the lights and siren. Thankfully, the suspect had slowed to a stop directly behind my car. I radioed to dispatch and the other officers en route that I had the suspect's vehicle stopped on Holloway Street.

I quickly jumped out of my patrol car and approached the suspect's silver car with my department handgun in my hands. A male located in the front driver's seat was the only individual I observed in the vehicle. I commanded the male to turn off the vehicle and to step out. A male in his early twenties with short blond hair wearing a white tank top and blue jeans obeyed and stepped out of the car. Fresh blood was running down from his nose and dripping on the front of his tank top.

I asked the male, Stanley, if he had had any weapons on him. Stanley said he didn't, but I patted him down just to be safe. The vehicle appeared to be empty. I asked Stanley where he was coming from and if anyone else was with him. He stated that he and his girlfriend, Tracy, had just left a friend's residence on Olive Street and were on their way home. He said nothing was wrong and that he and Tracy just had a small argument. Stanley informed me that there was no reason for me to pull him over because everything was fine now.

When I asked him how he got his bloody nose, Stanley stated that Tracy had struck him in the nose by accident, but he didn't want to file any charges against her.

While talking to Stanley, I smelled a strong odor of an alcohol emitting from his breath. Stanley's eyes were watery and bloodshot, and his speech was slurred. I asked Stanley where his girlfriend, Tracy, was. He informed me that she was fine and was just lying down in the backseat.

I placed Stanley in handcuffs and informed him he was being detained until I could determine that no crime had occurred. I asked Stanley again if he needed any medical treatment for his bloody nose, but he refused. Stanley stated that he did not want to file any charges against his girlfriend. He just wanted to take her home.

At that exact moment, another patrol car with its overhead lights and sirens activated came racing down Holloway Street towards us. The other police cruiser came to a screeching halt right next to where Stanley and I were standing by my patrol car and facing Stanley's vehicle.

Immediately, I radioed in to dispatch and to the other patrolman that I was secure and had the male suspect secured in handcuffs at this time. I did not want the responding units to think I was in danger or fighting with the suspect, which could cause them to drive recklessly or get involved in an accident due to the winter road conditions.

I turned to the other officer and asked him to watch the suspect whom I had detained in handcuffs. I cautiously approached the silver car, and I attempted to check on the female, Tracy, whom I still was unable to notice inside.

I opened the rear driver's side door, and I observed a horrific bloody scene. A female in her early twenties was lying across both backseats with her eyes closed and completely covered in dried blood. Blood was all over her face, in her hair, and all over the front of her white shirt. There was so much blood I could not indicate its source. Suddenly, Tracy's eyes popped wide open.

I asked her where she was bleeding at. Tracy, with a dazed expression, looked down at her shirt and seemed to not realize she was drenched in blood. I asked her again where she was bleeding. Tracy shook her head and said she wasn't bleeding. She stated that all the blood was from her boyfriend's bloody nose.

I had Tracy sit up on the backseat and asked her what had happened tonight. Tracy said her boyfriend, Stanley, had started drinking beer earlier in the evening at approximately eight o'clock at their friend's house, and he had just stopped drinking thirty minutes ago. It was now 2:30 a.m.

Tracy informed me that Stanley had become aggravated with her when she had talked to another guy. He began yelling at her. She stated that Stanley then told her they were leaving and grabbed her by her arm. He pulled her outside to his car. Tracy said she yelled at Stanley that she was not getting into the car with him because he was drunk.

She said Stanley then grabbed her by the neck, with an open hand, and attempted to shove her into the backseat of his car. Tracy said she began screaming at top of her lungs for help. She said Stanley shoved her into the car. He then got on top of her with both of his hands around her neck. Stanley was choking her to the point where she could not breathe or speak.

Tracy said she was able to raise her right leg up and kick Stanley square in the nose. Instantly, Stanley's nose began gushing out blood, and he quickly released his grip around her neck. She said she gasped for air and was relieved when Stanley released his hold on her neck. Tracy informed me that Stanley frantically jumped into the driver's seat and sped off.

Tearfully, Tracy stated she was so thankful that someone heard her cries for help and had called the police. Otherwise she had no idea what Stanley was going to do to her when they arrived home. She said she could not believe how quickly we responded to her aid, and she thanked me again.

When Tracy wiped away some of the dried blood from her face and neck, she showed me several red marks and scratches on both sides of her neck. She indicated that this was where Stanley grabbed her and attempted to choke her.

Ambulance personnel were dispatched to the scene and checked Tracy's vitals. Tracy refused to be transported to the hospital or to receive further medical treatment.

During this time, Stanley became arrogant and was cussing at the other police officer. He even attempted to bulk up and swing at the officer. You should never do this to an officer, but especially when handcuffed. It will not end well for anyone. Stanley ended up slipping on the snow-covered road and fell face-first to the ground without anyone touching him.

I shook my head as I assisted the other officer in helping Stanley back up onto his feet. I informed Stanley he was under arrest for domestic assault and driving while intoxicated. He was frustrated and continued to cuss during the entire ride. He repeatedly stated that he did nothing wrong and his girlfriend had kicked him in the nose.

When Stanley arrived at the jail, he had the audacity to say he was the real victim. He wanted to file charges against Tracy for kicking him in the nose.

Stanley was informed that everything would be documented in the police report. He was advised that it would be up to the prosecutor if any charges could be filed against his girlfriend, but at this time, he was the only one being charged for domestic assault and driving while intoxicated.

On a daily basis, law enforcement respond to domestic disturbances. Most of the domestics are only verbal, but occasionally, officers will witness physical abuse to the individuals involved.

When arriving at the scene, it's critical for all police officers to take control of the situation and separate everyone involved. Immediately separating individuals participating in the disturbance deescalates the fighting for a moment. After listening to both sides of the occurrence and examining evidence, the officer can confirm if a crime has occurred. After considering all the facts, the patrolman will immediately act by either apprehending the primary aggressor or giving a verbal warning to all the individuals involved. They may just need to remain separated for a few hours until all individuals calm down.

Main objectives for law enforcement after their strong determination to keep everyone safe is to prevent a crime from occurring. By assisting individuals to get out of an abusive relationship, patrolmen will advise them of helpful information on safe places, opportunities, and hotline numbers they can call. Ultimately, the choice is up to the individual involved; and sadly, too many times officers will respond back to an address for the same two individuals fighting.

All law enforcement officers have an unceasing determination to stop evil in its tracks and to help others. Patrolmen will continue to answer every call with integrity and professionalism even after responding multiple times to the exact same location for another disturbance.

EVENING JOY RIDE

It was a chilly Thursday evening in late September around ten o'clock. I was finishing up a traffic stop in the north part of town for exceeding the posted speed limit by ten miles per hour. The driver was polite and apologetic, and I released him with only a warning. When I informed dispatch that I was done with the traffic stop, they sent me to check the area of Medical Express in the south sector. Apparently, a motorist operating a four-door black passenger car was observed driving erratically in the Medical Express parking lot.

I responded to the location. I knew the Medical Express building had been closed since 5:00 p.m. Scenarios were running through my mind as I thought it could be juveniles driving around the parking lot doing donuts and pill outs.

Since it took about five minutes to get across town, I believed the suspect's vehicle would have been gone upon my arrival. I pulled into the large empty parking lot and stopped and checked the front door and windows of the building to make sure they were still secure and not damaged. Then I drove around the back of the Medical Express building to check the remaining exterior doors and windows.

All the doors and windows were secure, but I observed several fresh tire tracks in the grass located along the left side of the building and leading out into the field. Several plants along the edge of the parking lot and building had been destroyed by the vehicle's tires. Approximately ten feet from the parking lot, a small freshly planted tree had also been struck and was snapped in half. I located fresh tire tracks in the grass leading over the slight hill toward the woods, directly behind the building. Unable to observe where the lines ended, I decided to walk over the grassy hill to verify where the tire tracks led. I also had to determine if there was any more damage to the property.

As I parked my patrol car and secured it in the parking lot, I informed dispatch I was going to be out on foot patrol behind the business. I grabbed my flashlight off my duty belt and began the hike up the crest of the hill following the fresh tire tracks. After walking over the slight hill, I was able to see the entire bottom of the hill. Surprisingly, there was a black four-door passenger car stuck in the ditch at the bottom, near the woods.

I relayed to dispatch and the other officers by radio that I would be out with the suspect's vehicle. I quickly approached the vehicle, and I observed an older male in his late sixties sitting in the driver's seat. As I got closer, it became apparent that the car was stuck on a huge boulder underneath the driver's side tire.

Before I reached the front passenger side door, the engine loudly revved up, and the tire began spinning in place on the large rock. A loud squealing noise came from the front tire, and I could smell a strong odor of burnt rubber. Suddenly, several large sparks shot up from underneath the vehicle near the tire.

I ran up to the vehicle and tried to open the passenger side doors, but they were both locked. I banged on the front passenger window and attempted to get the driver's attention to inform him to turn off the vehicle. Surprisingly, the older male turned his head and looked right at me with a blank stare on his face. While looking at me, he slammed his right foot on the gas pedal, causing even more sparks to spray up from the rock. The driver's side tire continued to spin in place.

I was startled for a split second, but then a wave determination to save the man washed over me. Instantly, I knew I was going to do whatever it took to get the male out of the car before his vehicle caught on fire. I was gripping my flashlight in my hand. Without any hesitation and using the flashlight, I struck the window once with all my might. Miraculously, the window shattered and my hand went completely through it on the first strike. I was completely stunned because it normally takes several strikes to break a vehicle's window. This was my first attempt at breaking a window.

Before I could comprehend what I had done, I was reaching my arm into the vehicle and unlocking the front passenger door. I opened the door and stretched inside the car. I slammed the vehicle's gear shift into park. I turned off the vehicle and pulled the keys out of the ignition.

The older male, later identified as Graham, looked at me in disbelief with both of his hands held up in the air. His facial expression was shock and confusion. Graham mumbled several responses but was unable to answer my questions in complete sentences. He appeared confused about where he was or that his vehicle was stuck on a huge rock. I radioed to dispatch to have an ambulance respond to my location to do a medical check on the driver.

Within minutes, I heard loud sirens approaching and then observed an ambulance driving over the hill to our location. I assisted Graham out of the driver's side of the vehicle and handed him over to the paramedics. They walked him a few feet into the ambulance to check his vitals. It was discovered that Graham's blood sugar was extremely low, and he truly had no idea where he was or what was going on.

One of the paramedics approached me and asked me if I was all right. I gave him a strange look. He then said, "Didn't you break out the car window?" Then it hit me what I had done, and I examined both sides of my bare hand. Unbelievably, I didn't have even a scratch.

I was informed that the paramedics gave Graham something to eat to stabilize his blood sugar and he was going to be just fine. For precaution, Graham was being transported to the hospital to verify his blood sugar would remain stable. I was amazed and thankful we were able to locate Graham and get him the help he needed before it was too late.

Receiving this call, I automatically assumed it was juveniles out joyriding on private property. I would never have guessed it was someone in dire need of medical treatment. Honestly, I was glad I had a strong instinct directing me to continue looking for the suspect's vehicle and to follow the tire tracks over the hill. Unbeknownst to me, God was directing my steps the entire time and using me to find the individual and get him proper help. God puts the right people in our lives when we need them, and He is always protecting His people.

I am thankful God used me to accomplish His plan and will. This incident opened my eyes and proved God had always been looking after me and giving me the strength I needed to get the job done.

VICTIM OR SUSPECT

One October afternoon at approximately four o'clock, I responded to the police department in reference to a report of a robbery. Upon arrival, I contacted the victim, a nineteen-year-old female with shoulder-length blond hair, identified as Samantha. Immediately, I recognized her as being a suspect to several stealing and drug cases.

Samantha informed me that her friend, Natasha, had called her, asking her to come over. She said she told Natasha she would swing by before her appointment this afternoon. Samantha told me she had an appointment at 4:00 p.m. to meet her bail bondsmen to make a scheduled payment and that she had three hundred dollars' cash on her.

Samantha stated that at approximately 3:30 p.m., she pulled up in her car and parked it directly in front of Natasha's apartment duplex. Natasha's apartment was located approximately four blocks from the police department. Samantha said that Natasha's boyfriend, Ricky, a black male in his early twenties, jumped into the back passenger side of her car. Suddenly, another black male, identified as Kirk, age twenty-four, opened the front passenger door and sat down. Samantha stated she was startled, and before she could react or say anything, Kirk demanded her to give him all her money.

Samantha said she was paralyzed in the driver's seat, unable to move or react. She said Kirk demanded she pay him the money she owed him. Unexpectedly, Kirk then grabbed at her chest and kept reaching his hand into her bra and pulling down her tank top.

Samantha stated she attempted to swing at him with one arm and cover her chest with her other hand. Kirk then yelled at Ricky, sitting in the backseat, to hold her arms. Samantha stated she continued to struggle and swing her arms, but then Ricky grabbed both of her arms. She told me Ricky strongly held down both of her arms at her sides to the point where she was defenseless against Kirk. She said Kirk quickly reached again into her bra and retrieved all her cash. Samantha informed me she had three hundred dollars stuffed inside her bra to pay her bondsman, and now it was gone. She said all her friends knew that she carried her money concealed in her bra.

Samantha said she was yelling no and screaming for the men to let her go. She was unsuccessful at getting out of their grasp. She stated that once Kirk had grabbed all of her money, Ricky released his grip. Suddenly she said Kirk grabbed the back of her neck and forcibly shoved her head down toward her feet. Samantha told me Kirk growled that he should just kill her. She said Kirk then told her to wait right there. He was going to go get his gun and kill her.

Samantha stated that surprisingly, Kirk and Ricky exited her vehicle and fled toward Natasha's second-story apartment. At that exact second, Samantha informed me that she glanced at the apartment and saw Natasha standing outside at the top of the stairs near her front door. She said she did not know how long Natasha was outside, but she might have heard her yelling at the two men.

Samantha said she was truly terrified and believed Kirk was going to retrieve a gun to shoot her. She stated that Kirk was a known dangerous drug dealer for the area and for St. Louis, Missouri. She believed there was an active warrant out for his arrest. Samantha was extremely frightened for her life and said she stomped the gas pedal to get away. However, she said her tires spun in place, and she did a peel out on the road as she drove away from the duplex.

Samantha showed me several scratches and red marks all across her upper chest and around her neck. Her tank top was stretched out, and she had more red marks on the back of her neck. All her injuries corroborated what she had told me. Photographs were taken of all her injuries and placed into evidence.

Samantha said she felt this robbery was a set up from the beginning. She informed me she frantically called her bail bondsman and told him what had occurred. He advised her to come to the police department to file a report.

I knew that the victim, Samantha, had been arrested previously for possession of heroin. Now I was considering the possibility that the suspect, Kirk, probably knew Samantha carried drugs on her and could have been after them. I ran Kirk's information through our central communications center and was informed that he had an active warrant for his arrest for distributing illegal drugs.

After the interview with Samantha and gathering all the evidence, I went to Natasha's apartment to attempt to apprehend the two suspects. I arrived at the apartment with several officers, and we searched the premises. We were unable to locate Kirk and Ricky. After the search, I spoke to Natasha, an eighteen-year-old pregnant female with long black hair, and asked her where I could find Kirk and Ricky.

Natasha stated that her boyfriend, Ricky, and his friend, Kirk, were there about an hour ago, but had abruptly left her apartment without saying a word. She said she had no recollection of what had happened or where they had gone. I asked Natasha if she knew Samantha. She admitted she did and that her boyfriend, Ricky, told her to call Samantha and have her stop by for a minute. Natasha said that Ricky said he just needed to talk to her. She informed me she was unsure when Samantha had arrived, but when she stepped outside on her deck, she saw Samantha's silver car parked on the street in front of her apartment. Natasha saw Kirk and Ricky exiting the car. She said Samantha then spun her tires and sped off, but she was clueless to what had happened. Natasha informed me that Kirk and Ricky ran up the stairs to her apartment, grabbed the keys to her black Chevrolet Blazer, and dashed out to the car.

I passed on all the descriptive information about the two suspects and the vehicle to dispatch. Then I had dispatch place a stop and hold in the computer system for the wanted suspects and vehicle. So if any law enforcement officer contacted them and ran their information, the officer would immediately know to detain them for our police department.

Later that evening around ten o'clock, dispatch informed me that both of my suspects, Kirk and Ricky, had been located. They were being detained by police officers in St. James, Missouri, a small town less than fifteen minutes away. I radioed in to dispatch and stated that I was responding to their location. I escalated my speed while traveling on the interstate. I was shocked, and pleased, that the suspects were still in the area and did not flee to St. Louis or out of state.

When I arrived at the scene, I discovered that the suspects, Ricky and Kirk, had been pulled over on a traffic stop by the town's police officers. I separated the two suspects and spoke first to Ricky. After reading Ricky his Miranda rights, I asked him if he would be willing to talk to me. He agreed. When I asked Ricky to tell me what had happened this afternoon, he tried to deny knowing what I was talking about. I informed Ricky that I had a witness who had that observed him in Samantha's vehicle today; but I failed to tell him it was his girlfriend who had confessed.

The first words out of Ricky's mouth were that he had no idea it was going to go as far as it did. Ricky told me that his friend, Kirk, only mentioned that he needed to talk to Samantha about some money she owed him. Ricky said that when Samantha pulled up this afternoon in front of his girlfriend's apartment, he and Kirk both got into her vehicle. He stated he hopped in the backseat and Kirk jumped in the front. Ricky told me Kirk was demanding his money and began grabbing at Samantha. He stated Kirk then yelled at him to "hold her down."

Ricky informed me he did grab both of Samantha's arms while still sitting in the backseat because he did not want Kirk angry at him. He said he had no inkling what Kirk had in mind. Ricky stated he truthfully thought Kirk was just going to talk to Samantha and it would not get physical. He said they both released Samantha, exited the vehicle, and she quickly sped off.

Then I contacted Kirk and read him his Miranda rights. Kirk stated he understood his rights and agreed to talk to me. But when I asked him what had happened earlier that afternoon, Kirk acted like he had no idea what I was talking about. He denied knowing the female victim or laying hands on any female. Kirk said he never got into the female's car and had no idea why she would be accusing him of taking anything. He stated he never touched her and I could ask his friend, Ricky.

Smiling to myself, I did not inform Kirk that his friend, Ricky, had confessed to both of them being in the victim's vehicle and that Kirk was demanding money while grabbing at Samantha.

I placed Kirk under arrest for the robbery and for his active warrant for distributing illegal drugs. While searching Kirk, I was unable to locate the money taken from the victim. Ricky was also placed under arrest for the robbery, and I transported both suspects to the Phelps County Jail to book them.

Approximately a week later, I arrived at the local Town and Country grocery store for a report of a female shoplifter. Dispatch gave me a description of the blond female who was now exiting the store through the front entrance.

Surprisingly, it was Samantha, my robbery victim from last week. But now she was staggering around, unable to stand still, and had a very slow reaction time. It was apparent she was under the influence of narcotics.

When she saw me, Samantha quickly tried to throw a bright pink wallet pouch that matched her pink handbag into a trashcan outside. I laughed to myself because she really believed I didn't notice her attempting to hide her wallet in the trashcan. When I asked Samantha what she just threw away, she gave me a perplexed facial expression and began to look in the trashcan. Without hesitation, she reached into the trashcan and grabbed out an orange. She said, "Oh, just this orange."

I looked in the trashcan and was thankful to observe the wallet still lying on top of all the trash. I grabbed the wallet pouch and asked her what she had in it. Samantha said in a slurred speech, "That's not mine."

I opened the wallet and noticed several small clear baggies filled with a white powder, a spoon, a small digital scale, several syringes, and a lot of clear empty pill capsules inside it. The white powder tested positive for heroin, and the wallet pouch was the most organized heroin kit I had ever seen.

Samantha then admitted to stealing a book of stamps from the grocery store. She said she would gladly return them if I could release her. I placed Samantha in handcuffs and informed her I would ask the manager about the stealing charge, but she was under arrest for the possession of heroin and drug paraphernalia. After securing Samantha in my patrol car, I contacted the store manager to verify if they wanted to file charges. The manager stated that he did wish to file charges against the female for stealing, but would not request a trespass warning for the property at this time.

I transported Samantha to the police department and informed her she was also being charged for the stealing. Samantha pleaded with me not to charge her for the stealing because this was her third offense. In Missouri, it was an automatic felony charge on the third offense no matter the amount that was stolen. Samantha said she could pass on helpful drug tips and information about dealers if I would just take off the stealing charge. I informed her she would be allowed to speak to an undercover narcotics investigator about her facts. If the investigator found her information to be credible, he could ask the prosecutor to lessen or drop the charge.

One month later, I had to appear at the courthouse to testify on the robbery case involving Samantha, Kirk, and Ricky. Entering the courtroom, I observed Kirk, with shackles on his wrists and ankles, siting at the front desk next to the public defense attorney, facing the judge. Kirk was still incarcerated in the county jail and was wearing a black-and-white striped jumpsuit.

Directly across from the suspect sitting at the next table was Samantha, my victim for this particular case. Amusingly, she was wearing a bright orange jumpsuit from the county jail. Samantha, with shackles on her wrists and ankles, was also incarcerated on a separate charge.

Ironically, my victim was also a suspect, but had to testify as the victim in this case. This was a strange predicament and the first time I had ever witnessed in a courtroom. While testifying to the facts of the crime, the prosecuting attorney asked me if the suspect was in the courtroom and if I would point him out. I pointed to Kirk who was sitting up front in his black-and-white jumpsuit. Then I continued to answer questions fired from both the prosecutor and defense attorney.

Surprisingly, I later discovered that Samantha was trying to drop all the charges filed against Kirk and was saying how she had falsely accused him. The judge did not believe her and felt that Kirk was just trying to frighten her and her family. The judge ordered Kirk to be incarcerated in prison for twelve years.

Most police officers are not fond of court hearings because they are asked an abundant number of questions. Several defense attorneys attempt to get the patrolman flustered, aggravated, or find them at fault by catching them saying something that does not match their police report. At times, it certainly feels like the officer is the one on trial instead of the suspect who committed the crime. Some suspects refuse to testify and just remain in their front row seats, being disrespectful by glaring or smirking at the officers or victims.

DERANGED NAKED GUY

On May 6, 2012, it was a cool, breezy Friday night at 11:30 p.m. Dispatch broadcasted a report about a male, wearing nothing but his underwear, who was seen at the city park running across the parking lot. I was patrolling a few blocks from the park, so I informed dispatch I would be responding to locate the suspicious male. I thought this was unorthodox behavior with low fifty-degree weather. It was a tad too cold outside for anyone to be running around in only their underwear.

Within minutes, I arrived at the park and was circling around the lot checking for the suspicious male. It was pitch-black except for the illumination from the streetlights. I was unable to locate anyone, so I drove up the hill to the swimming pool parking lot. I cruised around the area with my windows down. I did not observe anyone or hear anything disturbing.

I turned around to complete another loop to verify that no one was hiding behind the playground equipment or trees. I approached a stop sign and came to a complete stop. While stopped, I heard a faint noise in the distance, which I believed to be glass breaking.

Attentively, I strained to listen, attempting to locate the exact location of the sound. *Smash!* There was the sound of glass shattering again. It seemed to be coming from a few blocks south of my location, somewhere on the right side of the street. Residences lined the entire right side of the road, and the park stretched across the left side.

Without warning, a loud high-pitched alarm tone echoed from my patrol car radio. Dispatch loudly announced that a burglary was in progress. They informed that an unknown male had shattered the victim's front window and was now attempting to smash through their front door. The address dispatch gave was only a couple of blocks south of my location. Automatically, I knew it was going to be one of the homes on the right side of the street across from the park.

I raced up the road and arrived at the victim's residence in record time. Shockingly, I observed a male in his early twenties, with short red hair, wearing nothing but a pair of dark-blue boxer shorts. It was the original male I was attempting to locate minutes earlier, who had been observed dashing through the park. The half-naked male was positioned in an aggressive stance facing the victim's front door. He gripped a short metal post above his head. He had already shattered all the glass in the front full-length storm door. There were several large triangle shards of glass along both sides of the door. I knew this was where the broken glass noises came from.

Immediately as I pulled up to scene, I saw the male suspect use the metal post and smash through the victim's front-door window. I quickly forced my patrol car into park and radioed into dispatch I was on the scene. I rushed toward the suspect and noticed that one of the house's front windows had been broken out. I immediately pulled my department Taser out of its holster and pointed it at the suspect. With the Taser's safety switch turned off, I aimed its red laser dot directly on the suspect's back. I demanded the male to stop and get on the ground.

The male, later identified as Steven, froze in place. He was in midswing with the metal post held above his head about to strike the victim's front door again. Steven slowly turned his head to look over at me. Steven had a cold, blank stare planted on his face, and his mouth was slightly open. He stared in my direction with a pair of crazy, wild eyes as if he seemed to be looking past me. Steven's cold facial expression never changed even when he noticed a police officer standing behind him. Standing in place like a violent evil statue, he still gripped the metal post in both of his hands high above his head.

Shivers ran up and down my spine when I experienced Steven's cold, heartless facial expression and demeanor. I paused for a brief moment, knowing I was the only police officer on the scene. The first thought that ran through my mind was what if the suspect threatened to kill or harm me or the victims with the metal post. The Taser would not faze anyone if they were under the influence of certain drugs that numb their sensory system. The Taser is a nonlethal weapon that fires two small metal dart-like barbs attached by wires and a battery. It delivers electric current to disrupt voluntary control of muscles, causing temporary neuromuscular incapacitation.

My second thought was that I would use lethal force deploying my gun to stop the suspect if I needed to protect others or myself from him. Steven's deranged, reckless actions alarmed me, and I did not believe he understood where he was or what he was doing. He defiantly seemed to be under the influence of a narcotic.

Abruptly, a heavyset shirtless male named Paul, from inside the residence, reached through the broken front door for the suspect. Paul unexpectedly grabbed Steven by both of his arms to stop him from swinging the metal post at his door again. I was startled at the sight of the home owner's sudden appearance through the front door, but then acted to put a stop to anyone getting hurt.

I commanded to Steven, "Put down the metal post now!"

Surprisingly, Steven obeyed and tossed the post to the ground. With my Taser still aimed at the center of his back, I ordered Steven to the ground and to put his hands behind his back. Swiftly, Steven complied and lay facedown on the ground and placed both of his hands behind his back. Still in disbelief that Steven was listening, I hastily ran up, grabbed his hands, and placed my knee in the center of his back near his neck. This arresting technique kept suspects from being able to get up abruptly or resist being handcuffed. I secured Steven in handcuffs to keep him from harming himself or anyone else.

During this time, several other police officers arrived on the scene. Steven was advised he was being placed under arrest for breaking and entering and destruction of property. I had an officer secure

Steven in a patrol car, as I went to verify if anyone was injured and to assess all the damages.

I spoke to the home owners, Paul and his wife, Dawn, in their midtwenties. They stated they had never seen the male suspect before in their life. Dawn was still in tears. They both told me that neither one of them had any idea why he was violently breaking into their home. Paul said he heard the front window being shattered, and before they could call the police, the suspect had moved to their front door. He stated that for an unforeseen reason, the male began frantically breaking out all the glass with the metal post in his hands.

Both Paul and Dawn were so grateful and relieved that I showed up as quickly as I did. They also said they were extremely thankful I was able to stop the suspect from entering their residence; otherwise, they didn't know what he would have done. Dawn said the male just appeared to be out of his mind, and she had no idea why he was coming after them.

While talking to the home owners, I noticed Paul had several long lacerations along both sides of his torso. He was slightly bleeding, and I asked him how he received the cuts on his stomach. Paul looked down with a confused expression on his face. He told me it must have been when he reached through the broken front door.

Ambulance personnel were called to the scene to check on the home owners' injuries. The male victim acknowledged he was not sure how he received the long cuts, but said it must have been when he reached through their front door's broken glass window and grabbed the suspect. Apologizing to me for his actions, he advised he was acting on adrenaline and had no inkling he got sliced along both sides of his stomach by the large pieces of glass.

I observed several large triangular pieces of glass hanging along all the edges of the door frame and also on the full-length shattered screen door. Outside, broken glass pieces spread across the concrete steps that led to their front door. I walked over to the smashed glass window and saw large pieces of glass lying outside under the window.

At this time, the suspect was about to be transported to the county jail by another patrolman. Before the officer left the scene, I asked him to take a photograph of Steven for my police report.

Further investigation revealed that the suspect, Steven, had been at the park and removed one of the signposts from the ground. He then rushed cross the street to the victim's residence and without any hesitation broke the window. Steven then abruptly shattered the front door and smashed out the glass to the front door. It was later discovered that Steven was a college student who had smoked some synthetic marijuana and had no recollection where he was or what he had done.

While at the jail, Steven became arrogant and irate. He failed to comply to the officer's or the jailer's commands and refused to calm down. After attempting to make several swings at the jailers, Steven was placed in a secure chair. He was strapped into the chair with soft restraints across both wrist and ankles so he could not harm himself or others.

The booking photo I received of Steven was a close-up of his face with a wide-mouthed grin and wild eyes. He was still secured in the chair. I chuckled to myself because this was one of the funniest arrest photos I had ever seen. The photograph definitely summed up the entire bizarre evening.

The next day while at the police department, I received a call from Steven's attorney who asked if they could collect their client's pants and wallet. I informed them Steven was not wearing any clothes, except for his boxer shorts, when we contacted him. I explained how Steven was not able to give us any information about where his clothes were or why he was running around half naked.

Three weeks later, I responded to the police department for a male who needed to be fingerprinted for his prior criminal charges. Upon arrival, I met with a young college student in his early twenties who was wearing glasses and had short red hair. I realized that he looked very familiar, but I could not place where I had seen him before. It was not until I saw his name on his driver's license that I realized who he was. You guessed it! It was Steven!

Here was a normal well-dressed polite college student who, because of one night of partying with synthetic marijuana, could have gotten himself killed. Honestly, he could have been shot by the home owners for breaking into their home or he could have been shot by officers if he had decided to charge anyone with the metal post.

Law enforcement officers are trained to stop a threat using deadly force. They aim for the center mass, which is the chest area because it is the largest part of the body. Some individuals under the influence of narcotics or who have a mental imbalance will charge an officer with a deadly weapon to kill them. The police will fire shots at them, but if the suspect feels no pain, they will continue to attack the officer, not realizing that they have been shot. It's a dangerous and deadly situation for any officer to encounter.

I am truly thankful I never had to fire my gun on anyone, but this was the closest situation where I thought I might have to do it. This was also my first experience arriving on a scene and witnessing a suspect breaking and entering a home in plain sight. Remarkably, I rushed into action, failing to hesitate or freeze in place, and made the arrest without waiting for backup.

Now as I recollect memories of all these true events and bizarre behaviors the criminals possessed, I truly feel very fortunate and blessed to never have been harmed while I protected and helped others. I now know I always had God as my protector, my strength, watching over me and walking beside me on every single call.

This entire scenario was just a great reminder how God is good and His love never fails.

8

UNFORGETTABLE AMBULANCE CALLS

Another duty of a law enforcement officer is to assist ambulance personnel. Officers make sure the individuals who are getting help do not become combative or aggressive with anyone. Most ambulance calls involve assisting patients onto a stretcher or walking them out to the ambulance so they can be transported for medical treatment.

However, on several occasions, officers would have to respond for individuals who had overdosed and, as a first responder, our job is to revive them. When the victims woke up after being unresponsive, they would violently start swinging, punching, and kicking anything near them. They are startled, alarmed, and furious to notice the police holding them down. Normally, the victim would have no recollection they had stopped breathing and refuse to go to the hospital for medical treatment. Unbelievable! When the person is conscious and alert, officers cannot force the individual to seek medical treatment. They can only recommend and pray the person seeks treatment and the help they need.

It's extremely heartbreaking and common to witness first responders save a person's life and then the victim acts as if nothing happened and they are fine. Unfortunately, these are the same individuals who did not learn a lesson and you respond back to their location for another overdose a week later.

All overdose calls are received as a serious risk because they could turn into a dangerous situation. A police officer's main responsibility is not only helping the unresponsive person, but also the safety of everyone involved. Sadly, every patrolman will experience the occasional loss of life when we could not bring back the victim. Then they have the heart-wrenching job of breaking the news to their family.

Police officers respond to an abundant amount of ambulance assists and calls for service over the years. It is the unusual, bizarre, unheard-of situations that make them unforgettable calls. These were some strange and odd events that I will always remember.

Bizarre Behavior

Starting my career as patrolman back in 2008 for the city of Rolla was an eye-opener! My first peculiar ambulance assist call has always remained in my memory. I was working the evening hours and responded to a call of a "check the well-being" of an eighteen-year-old female. Arriving at a small apartment, I contacted a male, age twenty, with short brown hair, identified as Ben standing outside.

Ben informed me that his wife Vanessa appeared to be very depressed ever since giving birth to their son just a week prior. He said she was becoming more isolated and distant from him and their child. Ben said he did mention it to his wife to try to get the help she needed, but she kept refusing any treatment. He stated Vanessa would continue to tell him she was fine and nothing was wrong.

Ben said he felt something was terribly wrong with his wife. He informed me he arrived home today at approximately 6:30 p.m. after work, and Vanessa seemed slow to respond and was acting abnormal. Ben said he would just like to get her checked out at the hospital to make sure nothing was mentally wrong with her.

Upon entering the apartment, I encountered an eighteen-year-old female with medium-length brown hair pulled back in a ponytail. This was Vanessa. She seemed unfazed by the appearance of police in her home and remained seated on her couch just staring straight ahead. Strangely, Vanessa also appeared to have no concern for her child who was left crying in his bed.

While talking to Vanessa, she was slow to respond to our questions. Several times she would refuse to comment and just stare off in the distance with a blank look on her face. Since Vanessa was unable to answer some of the standard questions to verify that she was safe, healthy, and did not need any further medical treatment, it was decided to have a doctor exam her.

When Vanessa did talk, I observed that her lips and entire tongue were dark blue. When I asked her how she received a blue tongue, she ignored me and glanced behind me with a blank stare.

An ambulance was dispatched to our location so we could transport her to the local hospital. Vanessa was compliant the entire time she was loaded into the ambulance. She lay back on the stretcher and was buckled in without struggling or saying a word.

Thinking the ambulance crew and Vanessa were secure, the officer and I left the scene. Just as I made the right turn to head back to the department, the alarm sounded on my car radio.

Dispatch stated the ambulance crew at the call I had just left was requesting immediate help. The female in the back of the ambulance was now combative and physically fighting with the paramedics. Hastily I circled around the block back to the apartment where the ambulance was located.

Rushing to the back of the ambulance doors and pulling them wide open, I observed Vanessa trying to pull both of her arms away from the paramedics so she could continue swinging. I jumped into the ambulance and grabbed Vanessa so we could strap her back onto the stretcher. We put restraints on both wrists and secured her legs with several buckles.

Surprisingly, Vanessa relaxed and lay still on the stretcher with her eyes closed, but we were not going to chance her becoming combative again. I talked to the other officer on the scene, and it was decided I would ride along in the back of the ambulance with the paramedic. This way, if she started struggling and tried to exit the ambulance, I could help keep her held down. The other officer said he would follow behind the ambulance in his patrol car just in case another situation occurred. Then the other officer would give me a ride back to my patrol car after we arrived at the hospital.

As the ambulance began to travel toward the hospital on the main highway, Vanessa opened her eyes and raised her head. Suddenly she decided she was not going to the hospital. She started trying to bite at her straps on her right wrist and attempted to pull her arms free. I grabbed Vanessa's left arm, and the paramedic grabbed the other. Thrashing her arms from side to side, she continued to struggle and attempted to squirm free. Vanessa then began struggling to raise both of her legs up out of the buckles. She was able to kick her left leg free of the strap.

During this time, the ambulance driver pulled over to the side of the road. Just before I could radio the officers that she was combative, the rear ambulance doors flew open. I saw the other officer standing in the open-door entrance. I was relieved to see an extra pair of hands hold down the wiry female.

Unexpectedly, Vanessa was able to get both of her legs free from all the buckles. The other officer swiftly grabbed both of her legs while she had them in midkick and continued to hold them down so she couldn't kick us. Vanessa then raised her head and tried pulling her left wrist to her mouth. She then attempted to bite my hand, but missed and bit her arm. I was startled at her bizarre actions, but I continued to hold her left arm down and told her not to bite herself.

I realized I had never seen anyone with a blank evil stare and large wild brown eyes before. We were able to secure Vanessa again to the stretcher and kept her from harming herself and anyone else.

Investigation revealed that Vanessa had been eating dried blue paint chips off a wall prior to officers arriving at her apartment. She now had no idea what she was doing or what was going on.

Suicidal Attempt

Another bizarre ambulance case I have never forgotten was a suicide attempt that failed. It was one o'clock in the morning, alarm tones pierced through the air, and dispatch was advising that a male had multiple self-inflicted stab wounds.

Rushing to the victim's residence with lights and sirens activated, patrolmen located the male victim, a twenty-year-old, lying on a couch in the living room. The male was shirtless, wearing only boxer shorts, lying on his back with his eyes closed. The male was unresponsive but still had a pulse. Looking at his chest, he had six deep lacerations in his lower stomach. One stab mark was in his chest.

While officers and paramedics tended to him, I contacted a female who was also in the home. The female advised it was her husband on the couch and he had stabbed himself with a kitchen knife. She told me her husband seemed upset when he came upstairs to their bedroom an hour earlier and told her goodbye. His wife said she thought it was odd behavior, but did not believe he was going to try to harm himself.

I spoke to the man's wife. She had no expression on her face, and her voice showed no emotion. It was like talking to a robot and a strange reaction to someone who just found their husband stabbed on the couch. The first thought that came across my mind was that she had stabbed her husband. I could not understand how you could care about a person, yet show no emotions when that person is seriously injured and might not live through the night.

The wife showed me where the kitchen knife was lying on the living room floor about eight feet from the couch. The knife had a black handle and a long six-inch blade and dried blood on the top of it. It was collected and placed into evidence.

Six of us loaded the man onto a stretcher. We carried him out of the house and down the steps. When we stepped on the second step, he suddenly raised up like a zombie and made a gagging noise. He turned his head toward my side of the stretcher.

This startled me. The man was making loud gagging noises like he was about to throw up. I stepped to the far-right side to be out of the way if anything did come up.

The man survived and told investigators that he had stabbed himself six times in the stomach. I could not imagine what would cause someone to try to end his life by stabbing himself with a long knife! That would be so painful, and you would have to be so dedicated to continue jabbing yourself.

I observed the male four months later as an employee at the hospital. As I walked past him, he had no recognition that I had witnessed him on that horrific painful night.

Midnight Escort

One midnight shift, I had to assist an ambulance crew transport a five-feet-two ninety-five-pound female, aged thirty-five, named Nikki, to a hospital approximately four hours away. The psychiatric hospital would be able to house the female patient for the duration of her treatment. Our local hospital did not have any rooms available in the psych ward.

Law enforcement officer's responsibility is to make sure the ambulance personnel and the patient are protected and safe during the entire trip. Officers also keep the patient from trying to harm themselves or exit the ambulance. Unfortunately, there have been several occasions when a patient suddenly decided they did not want to receive help and attempted to flee from a moving ambulance.

This was the first time I had ridden a long distance in the back of an ambulance; I was not sure how I was going to handle the car ride. Consequently, I have gotten nauseous on long car rides on curvy roads. Remarkably, after the four-hour transport, I was able keep my stomach from getting nauseous. Only a few times I had to look toward the ambulance's front windshield since there were no side windows in the back. During the ride, Nikki was relaxed and buckled onto the stretcher. She was quiet and slept the entire time.

When we arrived at the hospital, I had to wake Nikki and inform her we had arrived. She sluggishly walked into the hospital without any arguments or disgruntled behavior. I was thinking to myself that she appeared perfectly normal. How could she need psychiatric treatment?

Abruptly before entering the hospital doors, Nikki turned to me and asked me to help her. Giving her a confused expression, I asked why she needed help.

She stared at me with a blank stare and said, "Can you cut it out?" I was shocked and puzzled by this and asked "Cut what out?"

With a serious facial expression and without blinking, Nikki said, "The baby."

Here was a tiny thin female who did not appear to be pregnant. I was confused and asked her, "What baby?"

Without warning, Nikki raised her tee shirt and pointed to her flat stomach, saying, "This one." I gave her a perplexed look. Nikki seriously stated that an alien had impregnated her while she was sleeping and she needed to cut it out before it grew.

I honestly had no response to her peculiar question. As we entered the hospital, I informed Nikki that she was at the right place for help and that the hospital staff were going to take good care of her.

After dropping Nikki off with all her personal belongings, I had to just shake my head. I have heard some strange things in my career, but never about an alien impregnating someone. Amusingly, I started to think the female was being transported to the psych ward by mistake until she began speaking.

Feisty Fighter

It was a September evening at nine o'clock, and I was responding, with lights and sirens, to an unresponsive female located near the subway along the side of the road. Upon arrival, I located the female, with short red curly hair, lying on her stomach with her legs slightly sloped down the hill with a creek at the bottom. I rushed over to the female and rolled her onto her back to verify if I could feel a pulse.

Immediately, I recognized the five-foot-tall heavyset unresponsive female as Rebecca. She had several prior arrests for peace disturbances and physical domestic assaults against her husband. Remarkably, Rebecca was breathing, but was still unresponsive.

Ambulance personnel arrived on the scene and assisted me at pulling Rebecca up the hill near the sidewalk so we could load her onto a stretcher. While moving her up the slight hill, her left tennis shoe slid off her foot and rolled toward the creek. Luckily, I was able to grab the shoe before it went into the water.

The ambulance crew began lifting Rebecca onto a stretcher and giving her sternum rubs and smelling salts. These attempts are to help patients become alert and responsive, especially if drugs or alcohol are in their system.

Rebecca immediately began groaning and slowly opening her eyes. Regrettably then, the fight was on. For being only five-foot-tall and two hundred pounds, Rebecca was swinging her arms with closed fists and frantically kicking both of her legs like a skilled ninja. Everyone grabbed an arm or a leg and attempted to calm her down so she would not hurt herself.

Rebecca continued to struggle, cuss, and pull away. Finally, she began to simmer down slightly, and we were able to quickly place restraints on her wrists and ankles. Unfortunately, for Rebecca, securing her to the stretcher was the safest way to transport her to the hospital.

Then Rebecca passed out on us again. We woke her again, but this time she was unable to swing and kick. Ambulance personnel told Rebecca how we had to keep her conscious and alert since we were unaware of what type of narcotics she had taken.

I followed behind the ambulance in my patrol car to make sure they arrived safely at the hospital. Upon arrival, paramedics stated that Rebecca attempted to go unconscious, but they were able to wake her without an incident.

I helped escort Rebecca into the emergency room and informed the nurses the reason we had to restrain her. Every time she woke up, she would become physically combative. Before I left the hospital, I heard the nurses ordering the ambulance personnel to remove all the restraints.

I left the emergency room in disbelief because I knew I would be called back for Rebecca fighting with nursing staff. No surprise that a half hour later, I had to respond back to the hospital to take a police report. An ER nurse wanted to file charges against Rebecca for kicking her hard in the nose. The nurse did have a bloody nose.

Investigation revealed that the nurse was attempting to hook up Rebecca's IV in her right arm. Suddenly, Rebecca raised her right leg up toward her right arm and struck the nurse in her nose. The nurse was furious! The question I was wondering about was why the restraints were removed when the patient was known to be combative with law enforcement. Rebecca will definitely be remembered as a kicking, swinging, punching feisty ninja.

Stabbed Victim

It was a relaxing sunny June afternoon at two o'clock without many calls for service. I had one hour to go before I could go home and enjoy the nice weather outside. Unfortunately, that's when the alarm sounded on my portable radio. Dispatch stated that a neighbor reported hearing a male and female fighting in the next-door apartment. We were advised they heard loud banging, glass breaking, and screaming.

I ran out to my patrol car parked in the police department parking lot and activated my overhead lights and sirens. I rushed to the apartment duplex. I located the hidden road directly behind the Sonic restaurant. I turned off my lights and sirens in order to not allow anyone to know I had arrived.

As I approached the first apartment, I observed a five-feet-eight slender intoxicated female with stringy blond hair, aged forty-six, identified as Patsy, exiting the residence with her purse. I radioed dispatch and informed them I had arrived on the scene and would be out of the car with one of the involved individuals.

I immediately recognized Patsy from prior disturbance calls. She was always loud and obnoxious and very scantily clad. There had been numerous accounts when I had to instruct Patsy while she was intoxicated to cover herself because she always wore tank tops without a bra.

As I talked to Patsy, she informed me that everything was fine now. She stated that she and her boyfriend, Marvin, had gotten into an argument, but she was leaving now. I asked if she was injured anywhere, and she told me she was not. I informed Patsy I needed to contact her boyfriend before either individual could leave. Patsy began to become agitated and saying she did nothing wrong and that she was leaving.

I informed Patsy that she was being detained until I could verify that no crime had occurred, and I placed her in handcuffs. I secured her in the back of my patrol car and knocked on the front door of the residence. I heard a faint voice coming from inside the residence.

As I opened the door, I observed a male, identified as Marvin, in his fifties sitting back on the couch with no shirt on. Marvin looked at me and said, "The crazy *beep* stabbed me." He leaned forward and showed me a slight laceration in his back. Quickly, I radioed into dispatch to have an ambulance respond to my location for a male victim who had been stabbed.

Marvin informed me that his girlfriend, Patsy, got mad at him for talking to another female at work and began screaming at him. He told me he called her a "crazy b———h" and turned his back to her. Marvin said that the next thing he knew, he felt a piercing sharp pain in his shoulder. When he turned around, he noticed a metal nail file sticking out of his back. Marvin said he could not believe she stabbed him. He stated that he demanded she get out of his apartment. That was when we pulled up.

Paramedics arrived on the scene and transported Marvin to the hospital. I then approached Patsy and had her tell me what had really happened today. Patsy at first tried crying and saying Marvin was always abusive with her. She said about how he became angry with her and she was just defending herself. Patsy tried to say she was in fear for her life and that was the reason she stabbed him.

When I asked Patsy why she had to stab her boyfriend in the back if she was defending herself, she realized I was not believing her phony description. Patsy became irate, cussing and demanding that I let her go. She stated how he deserved it and she should have stabbed him several more times to stop him from talking. I was still unsure what caused Patsy to snap and stab someone. But I did know she would be spending a few years in prison for her actions.

One must realize that every call for a police officer or first responder could be dangerous and bizarre. Honestly, officers seldom know the individuals that they encounter on a daily basis or their state of mind. Patrolmen do their jobs professionally, attempting to get to the truth of every situation and try to help others if they will allow us.

PARENTS NOT PARENTING

Every police officer is unique. As an officer, you have your own style of how you handle calls, type reports, keep your desk, and wear all your issued police gear on your duty belt. No two officers are alike.

But there is one circumstance where most patrolmen would agree. If you would ask any officer what is one thing they despise to hear a parent say to a child, they would tell you it's when the parent says, "You see that police officer? They are going to arrest you if you don't behave."

Realistically, an officer will hear this several times in their career. Whether the adult is joking or being serious, it is not a good idea to say this to a child. This is teaching children if they do anything wrong, they will automatically be arrested. Then the child is filled with fear or becomes afraid of the police.

Parents should instead tell children that the police are their friends and are there to help them or anyone else who needs help. As a parent, you are establishing how you want your children to behave, and they are intensely watching and listening to your every word.

Personally, I strongly believe children should be raised to obey their father and mother. This gives all children a strong foundation of morals and respect for others and themselves.

I also agree that all children need to be taught about the Lord and the ultimate sacrifice He went through so we could be forgiven of our sins and have eternal life. If a child does not learn about the Lord, they grow up not knowing Him or having a true loving relationship with our Heavenly Father. Sadly, they start living a selfish life, only looking out for themselves and wanting material gain or money. This type of life turns individuals into having insecurities, depression, anxieties, or addictions. I know this from personal experience.

Honestly, I was raised not knowing anything about the Lord. My family never went to church. I grew up believing in God, but I had never read the Bible or heard of Resurrection or Palm Sunday. In October 2017, at the age of thirty-four, I began going to church for the first time. I learned about all the Bible stories many children learn when they are younger. I am truly thankful and blessed God had called me to have fellowship with Him and the church.

No Parental Control

One warm summer night in July, at approximately 11:00 p.m., I had just begun my midnight shift. Before I even checked my e-mails or phone messages at the department, I was being dispatched to an apartment duplex. The apartment duplexes were located directly past the Interstate 44 overpass. Dispatch was saying that a young child was seen running around the apartment's rear parking lot wearing nothing but a diaper, with no adult present.

Arriving at the duplex I drove all the way to the rear apartments to see if I could locate the young child. As I pulled my patrol car into a vacant parking spot I observed a five-year-old boy wearing nothing but a diaper, on the left side of the parking lot.

Slowly approaching the child, I told him I was a police officer and I was there to help him. The little boy just stood there, giving me a puzzled expression, staring at me and not saying a word. As I approached the child, I looked around for an adult who would be watching him. I was unable to see anyone outside. I asked the juvenile where his mommy or daddy was.

The five-year-old gave me a huge grin and took off sprinting across the parking lot toward the apartments. I raced after the child and saw him quickly run up a flight of stairs to the second-story apartments. Before I could reach the top of the stairs, I heard the juvenile run into an apartment and shut the door. A sense of dread came over me because there were six apartments on the second floor, and I was unable to see which apartment number he had run into.

As I reached the top of the staircase, I could hear a cat hissing and growling down the hall. I glanced in the direction of the noises and noticed a black tail wedged in between an apartment door and frame. I realized the little boy had slammed the door shut on the poor cat's tail! Suddenly the child opened the apartment door so the cat would get its tail inside the house. When he saw me, he slammed the door shut again.

I was not sure if this was the child's correct address, so I informed dispatch the apartment number where I would be at. I loudly knocked on the door, but got no response. I tried the door handle. Remarkably, the door was unlocked, and it opened slightly. I noticed a male passed out on the couch located in the living room.

I had to wake up the man, named Chris, to verify that the child lived there. He sluggishly woke up and seemed only slightly confused to have a police officer standing in his living room. I informed Chris there was a five-year-old boy that was located outside who ran into this apartment. He said that was his son, who was autistic. Chris said his son could not fully speak yet. I told him his son was outside running around the parking lot with no one watching him, wearing nothing but his diaper. Chris told me he had a hard time keeping his son in the apartment because he knew how to open doors. I asked him if there was anyone else who could help keep an eye on his son. He told me the boy's mother had left them a week ago to get drugs and had not returned home. Chris said this was not the first time the child's mother had left them.

While talking to Chris, I smelled a moderate odor of alcohol on his breath. I concluded this was why he did not hear me knocking on the front door.

I informed the boy's father that he needed to do something so his child would not open the front door and run around outside near the streets. I advised him of the dangers of cars or the possibility of being kidnapped. I informed Chris that it was Missouri state law that I had to hotline tonight's events with him and his son to the Division of Family Services. He was advised DFS would be doing a follow-up investigation to make sure there was a safe environment for the child and that no other dangerous occurrences had happened. The child's father said he understood and he would make sure it did not happen again.

Approximately forty-five minutes later, I responded to the police department for a report of a young juvenile found walking in the road. As I arrived at the scene, I contacted a young college couple holding the same five-year-old boy from the earlier report. I was astonished to see the five-year-old still wearing only a diaper. His father was nowhere in sight.

The couple informed me that at 11:45 p.m., they were traveling past the apartment duplex toward the Interstate 44 entrance ramp. They observed this young boy walking along the side of the street. The female said she became frightened for the child who was getting extremely close to the road. She said she was scared for the boy's safety, believing he would get hit by a car if he made it onto the interstate. The couple stated, thankfully, they were able to grab the little boy before anything terrible happened to him. They told me they were not able to locate anyone around the area, so they brought the child straight to the police department. They said they could not understand how anyone could allow their five-year-old to be outside in the middle of the night walking near the streets.

I thanked the couple for being Good Samaritans and doing the right thing for the child. Miraculously, the child was picked up by good, honest people who did not want to see any harm come to him.

As the couple left the department, I carried the juvenile back to my office. I called the child's father, Chris, to tell him we had his son. I discovered he had fallen back to sleep after we had left and had no inkling that his child was gone. Chris also failed at putting a temporary object against the door to alert him if the juvenile attempted to escape again. I was frustrated with Chris's lack of concern for his son's safety. I informed him I would be contacting the Division of Family Services and that an agent would be responding to his residence tonight.

I then called the DFS and told them what had just occurred for the second time within an hour. They agreed that it was not a safe environment for the child to return home. A DFS agent arrived at the police department to see the child, and then we went over to the apartment. DFS told the father that the child was being placed in temporary care of the State until a court hearing could be scheduled. During that time, both parties could plead their case in front of a judge.

I had been in law enforcement for over ten years, and that was the first time I witnessed such an unsafe living situation for a young child. Two months later, I had to appear at court for the hearing to testify as a witness for the State of Missouri. The prosecuting attorney informed me I was not needed to testify on the case and the juvenile's mother had won full custody of the child. Unfortunately, it was unclear if this was going to be a better living environment for the child.

Assisting Division of Family Services

Police officers are called daily to help assist Division of Family Service (DFS) agents on their investigations. Every time DFS receives a hotline call, they have forty-eight hours to do a follow-up interview with the children and family members to verify if the accusations are true. Most of the hotline tips are false claims due to disgruntled family members.

Protocol for DFS agents is to always have an officer present on all investigations for safety. DFS agents have the daunting task of contacting families about the accusations and then verifying that corrections had been made for the safety of the child or children involved. A lot of adults would become agitated, upset, angry, and hostile. The police officer's presence was not only for the safety of the Division of Family Service agent, but also to keep the peace between everyone present. Understandably, if there was a risk of harm or death for the children, then steps would be taken right then to have them removed from the home.

On one Division of Family Service call, which I assisted, the girl's eighteen-year-old boyfriend became irate that we were at their residence. The boyfriend started yelling and cussing at us to leave and refused to settle down. I calmly explained to him that the DFS agent had a job to do, and he needed to calm down or he would be placed under arrest for interfering with an investigation.

The boyfriend looked at me and said, "You better place me in handcuffs because I am not going to calm down." Nodding my head, I said, "Okay. Turn around."

Amazingly, he complied and placed both of his hands behind his back. I placed him in handcuffs and informed him he was not under arrest, he was just being detained for the moment.

The man said he understood and simmered down quickly so the handcuffs were removed. I thought to myself that I should have done that at the beginning. For some reason, he was unable to tone down his anger until he understood the consequences of his actions.

As a police officer, my responsibility is to defuse all altercations and take control of every situation. It is a lot of stress and responsibility placed on one person whom you have just met. But knowing you can help one person or change one life for the better makes it all worth it.

One of my hardest Division of Family Services assist calls was when I had to remove three young children, all under the age of ten, from their home. No officer wants to take children from their family, but if it keeps them safe, we have no problem doing it.

I responded to an apartment where I met up with a DFS agent. The agent informed me that the mother of the three children had just given birth to another child and was still at the hospital. She stated that the mother had tested positive to methamphetamine and cocaine in her system. Sadly, the newborn baby also tested positive for methamphetamine in its system.

The DFS agent told me they had to remove the newborn baby from the mother and the State of Missouri was awarded custody of the baby. She informed me that the father recently took a drug test, and he tested positive for cocaine. Shockingly, she said we were there to remove all three children from the home.

When I arrived at the apartment, the children's father opened the door. I informed him of the reason we were there. Surprisingly, the father knew he was not going to pass the drug test and began sobbing. I gave him time to hug his children and then helped him get some clothes and belongings together. Witnessing the entire event was heart wrenching and painful to see three young children to experience. My feelings then turned into anger and rage toward the father. I could not fathom how a father would choose doing drugs over keeping his three children.

As I glanced around the spotless apartment, it was cleaner than most residences where I had been. Personally, I hated to have to take the children away from their family. Ultimately, I wished both parents could have stayed away from the illegal drugs, if not for them, then at least for their children.

As an officer, you have an obligation to make sure everyone is safe, especially children who cannot protect themselves or who don't know any better. Ten years into my law enforcement career, and this was the first and only time I had to physically remove children from their home. It's not a day anyone can easily forget, but you continue to hope and pray for a better life for all the children involved.

BAR FIGHTS

Patrolmen responding to a bar fight already know it can be a risky, dangerous, and unknown situation. Therefore, more than one officer will always be dispatched as backup to the same location. When individuals are intoxicated, angry, and surrounded by glass bottles, you can presume what happens next. Police officers are responsible for the safety of everyone, even the individuals who started the physical altercation.

Unfortunately, those intoxicated individuals can and sometimes do choose to take their frustrations out on the officers. Most law enforcement officers find responding to bar altercations as an adrenaline rush. Nothing gets your heart rate accelerated like rushing to a scene with lights and sirens to help others. Here are a couple of bar fights and altercations that I remembered over the years.

On an early Saturday morning, at 2:00 a.m., I was en route, with several officers, to a local bar for an intoxicated male causing a loud disturbance and trying to fight with several patrons inside the bar. The bar was located on the corner of a busy street in the downtown district.

I pulled up in front of the bar and located an intoxicated male in his early twenties staggering around outside the bar. The male appeared to be attempting to push his way past an employee who was standing in front of the business's door. The employee had his arms folded in front of him and was not allowing the intoxicated male into the bar.

I separated the intoxicated male from the employee and had him stand on the sidewalk away from the front door. During this time, the police sergeant arrived on the scene and began talking to the intoxicated male. After making sure the sergeant was secure, I spoke to the employee to make sure no one was injured.

The employee advised he had been working security tonight at the bar when the intoxicated male continued to cause a disturbance by yelling, cussing, and being obnoxious toward other customers. The employee informed me that the intoxicated male then became agitated and tried to punch several individuals for no apparent reason. He stated that they escorted the male out of the bar before anyone was injured. The employee informed me that they did not wish to file charges against the male, but they wanted him to leave the premises.

I walked over to the edge of the sidewalk near the city street where the sergeant and another police officer were talking to the intoxicated male, Chris. The sergeant asked Chris if he knew someone we could call to come give him a ride home. Chris was being uncooperative and demanding to know why we were harassing him.

The sergeant asked Chris for his identification to verify he did not have any warrants for his arrest. Chris sluggishly took out his wallet from his back right pocket. When the sergeant went to reach for Chris's wallet, he quickly pulled it away from the sergeant's grip, ripping it out of his hand.

Unexpectedly, Chris gave the sergeant a furious glare and bulked up his chest. The sergeant told him not to even think about it. Before we knew what was going on, Chris took a wide swing with his right fist at the sergeant's face. Remarkably, the sergeant was able to swiftly step back out of the way. Chris missed the sergeant entirely and almost fell on his face.

The other six-feet-four police officer attempted to grab Chris by his arms, but he continued to squirm and pull away. The officer quickly tried to Tase Chris, but his Taser malfunctioned. Chris continued to vigorously flail his arms and charged toward the sergeant. The other officer and I each grabbed an arm and forcibly escorted

Chris to the sidewalk, unfortunately directly in front of the bar's front door.

Chris was deliberately lying on both of his arms and keeping them tucked under his chest. He refused to give us his arms and would not comply to any orders. I was trying to grab Chris's right arm while the other officer held him down by the back of his neck. The sergeant held down his legs. A university officer rushed to our aid and attempted to grab Chris's left arm.

Chris was cussing at us to "get the f——k off." He continued to refuse to give us his arms. We used pain compliance to have Chris obey our orders. I attempted to pull his right arm from underneath him and at the same time used the back of my flashlight to strike the side of his stomach. Then the sergeant used his Taser and drive stunned Chris along his inner thigh.

During this time, several intoxicated individuals were trying to exit the bar's front doors. I ordered them to shut the door and go back inside. Since it was uncertain if they were Chris's friends coming to help him, it was safer to keep everyone inside.

Finally, Chris followed orders and placed both of his hands behind his back. After placing him in handcuffs, we had paramedics check him. After the paramedics released him, he was transported to the county jail.

The next day, I discovered that Chris's mother was a correction officer who worked in the jail. I was glad to hear she did not work the night before so she didn't have to witness her son intoxicated and placed in jail.

Drunk Female on the Run

A cold November Saturday morning at one thirty, I was traveling past a bar on the west side of town. The bar was located off Kings Highway, just diagonal from a gas station next to the Interstate 44 entrance ramp.

I saw a known female, Megan, in her early twenties, whom I had arrested before on active warrants. She was staggering out of the bar. Megan looked toward the patrol car with a concerned expression on her face and turned around quickly.

I ran Megan's information through our system and was informed she had an active warrant for failure to appear on a stealing charge. I turned the car around and went to contact Megan. Pulling into the bar's gravel parking lot, I observed her make a quick dash for the woods located directly behind the bar. Before I could exit my car, she ran into the woods.

I knew the woods flowed across the back of the businesses and hotels on the right side of the highway. Instead of running blindly through the trees and brush, I drove my car to a hotel parking lot about a half block over and parked it. I knew the woods thinned out behind the hotel, and I just waited and watched for Megan to exit the woods.

A few minutes later, there was Megan walking out of the woods and crossing the lawn of the hotel. She must have thought she had gotten away because she was walking calmly. I approached her from along the side of the hotel and told her to stop where she was.

Megan gave me a startled look and then ran toward the highway. I ran after her and radioed into dispatch that I was in foot pursuit of a female suspect headed toward the park on Kings Highway. Megan then darted across the highway without even slowing her stride. Thankfully, there was not much traffic and she made it across without being struck by a vehicle.

I raced after Megan, closing the distance between us. She ran to the park and hid behind the first bare shrub. There were no leaves on the shrub to conceal her. I had to laugh because she really believed I could not see her hunkered down behind the twig bush.

I pulled out my Taser and told the female to get on the ground, or I was going to Taser her. Surprisingly, she complied and lay face-down on the ground. I came up behind Megan and placed her in handcuffs. Megan said, in a slurred speech, that she could not believe how fast I was. I smiled to myself because she had no idea I drove to the location.

I informed dispatch I had the female suspect in custody. I advised dispatch and the other officers that I was secure and they could slow their response. During this time, an officer and a sheriff's deputy arrived at my location. Our dispatcher confirmed Megan did have an active warrant for stealing. While the officers were watching her for a brief moment, I ran across the street and grabbed my car.

When I returned to the officers and the intoxicated female, I was told how Megan would not stop talking. The officers were relieved that I was putting her in my patrol car and transporting her to jail.

While transporting Megan to jail, she still could not comprehend how I had run so fast. She said she didn't see me chasing her. Megan told me she thought she had gotten away when she ran through the woods.

Two years later, I responded to a residence for a report of stealing. As I arrived at the scene, I observed a female whom I recognized. It was Megan. She was politely telling me how she was staying out of trouble and showing up to all her court dates. Megan also told me she had not run from the police since that night. As I was leaving the residence, I overheard Megan telling another male, "Don't run from that cop. She is fast!"

I smiled to myself as I remembered that night. I had never mentioned to Megan that I had driven my car to the hotel parking lot that night she ran from me. She assumed I had continuously chased her from the bar through the woods.

Hopefully, Megan learned her lesson that it is never wise to run from the police. That will only add on more charges and jail time to your sentence. Eventually, the police will always locate their suspects.

Fraternity Party

Most police officers work a lot of overtime, signing up for security or traffic details. I would request to do a lot of these assignments. The traffic details consisted of using your patrol car to block of a section of road for several hours or running nonstop traffic stops for four hours.

However, security assignments for the college fraternity parties were normally uneventful. Officers were usually asked to stand outside near the entrance doors and check identifications no matter the type of weather. Unfortunately, the last security detail I worked turned out to be an unpredictable, ridiculous, chaotic turn of events.

It was the last week of June in 2015 on a Friday night. Another officer and I were assigned to a huge dance competition held at a VFW south of town. Unbeknownst to us, more than two hundred individuals from St. Louis, Missouri, would be arriving to this event.

All the individuals crowded the front entrance door and failed to form a single line. While trying to organize the chaos at the front doors, the president of the fraternity, Shawn, came outside and was ushering several individuals past us to go inside. We informed Shawn we had not checked their identification, and he told us, "It's okay. They're with me." The other officer and I both shook our heads. We continued doing our job through the mass confusion and tried to keep others from pushing their way through.

While standing outside, I was approached by a young Asian couple. The couple said they were not sure if they were at the right fraternity party. They asked me if I had observed anyone of their kind going inside. Shaking my head, I informed them they might want to verify the address to make sure they were at the right location.

Looking at the enormous crowd still gathered at the front entrance, I noticed all the females wearing tight skimpy dresses with the tallest stilettos. All the males wore tee shirts and baggy jeans. Occasionally, an individual would walk past us to enter the building and you could smell a hint of freshly smoked marijuana. We just shook our heads because we knew they could not be arrested for smelling like marijuana.

During this time, a male ran outside the front doors and yelled, "They're fighting!" The officer and I rushed into the banquet hall. It appeared to be full to capacity already. There were people on every inch of the dance floor. As I pushed toward the center of the floor, I heard people yelling, "Hurrah!" and a mob dance group broke into a coordinated stomp routine with claps. I was startled for a second, but I stopped and realized they were only dancing and not physically fighting.

As I glanced around the dark room, which only had laser and strobe lights flashing, I saw Shawn knocked out on the floor with his arms still raised slightly in the air. I then observed a large six-feet-two 250-pound shirtless black male, named Henry, being held against the wall by five other males. Henry had a furious facial expression, and his friends were telling him to calm down. He continued to try to pull away from their grasp so he could go after Shawn who was still unconscious lying on the floor.

Getting in Henry's face, I yelled over the loud music for him to get out and pointed toward the door. As he began to walk toward the front doors, Shawn woke up, swinging his fists, trying to strike anyone near him. I turned my attention to Shawn and ordered him to calm down before he injured an innocent bystander. When Shawn had realized where he was and that the police were standing in front of him, he calmed down.

I then exited the VFW and followed Henry outside with the other officer behind me. I informed Henry that he was to leave the property. Then Shawn crashed out the front doors. He said everything was fine now and Henry was welcome to come back to the party. In disbelief, I informed Henry that he was not allowed back into the building due to the physical altercation or he could be arrested. Thankfully, Henry complied and left the premises with another friend without any further incidents.

Surprisingly, we then had two more altercations inside the building and called for other officers to assist us. As we rushed back into the VFW, we discovered that all the fighting individuals had been separated and asked to leave the property. While escorting the individuals outside, I observed three police officers who were stuck behind the large herd of people. Shockingly, they were still trying to squeeze past them to get into the building, but no one was moving out of their way.

I was furious to think, if we immediately needed help, none of the officers could get to us quickly. There were no precautions set up for our protection or safety. Deciding this was enough, we abruptly shut down the party and had everyone leave. We had State Highway Patrol, sheriff's deputies, and our officers arrive at our location.

Shawn was furious that we were forcing the fraternity party to be shut down early, and he was vocally stating his disappointment. He yelled how we had no right to stop their party. Then a female was walking toward the front doors and gave me a disgusted look and kept mumbling rude comments under her breath. I walked behind her, making sure everyone exited the VFW safely.

I was relieved to see this violent chain of events coming to an end for the night. I saw that it was only midnight. It felt a lot later in the morning, and I was exhausted. Technically, we were scheduled to work the security detail until 3:00 a.m., but we both were glad to be done.

Remarkably, out of all the security details I had done in the past ten years, this was the only time an organization was forced to shut down early due to all the disruption and physical altercations. All I could do was shake my head and think to myself, "No more fraternity parties for me." I had worked my last one.

Robbery in Progress

It was a warm Sunday morning around ten o'clock, on April 20, 2014. I had just exited the police department and gotten into my patrol car. Unexpectedly, a loud alarm went off on my car's radio. Dispatch stated a robbery had just occurred at Lowe's, and the male suspect had fled the store on foot. The suspect was described as a twenty-year-old white male with buzzed red hair, wearing a gray hooded sweatshirt and blue jeans.

I activated my lights and sirens and responded to Lowe's. As I arrived at the business, I scanned the parking lot and drove around looking for anyone fitting the suspect's description. I was unable to locate the male so I went and spoke to the witness at Lowe's loss prevention department.

The employee, John, stated he noticed an unknown male in his early twenties acting suspicious while in the store. John said the suspect continued to oddly look around so he followed him through a few aisles. He stated he saw the suspect conceal a cordless drill underneath his gray hoodie. John informed me that the male then walked down another aisle, looked around, picked up a small item off the shelf, and concealed it in his shirt. He stated the suspect then made his way to the front of the store passing all the registers without paying for his concealed merchandise. John told me he then exited the store's front doors with the stolen items.

John informed me he approached the male outside and asked him for the unpaid-for merchandise. He stated surprisingly the suspect shook out his hoodie and several tools fell onto the ground in front of him. John said the male then pulled out a pocket knife and thrashed it toward him.

John said he was startled that the man would attempt to use force after he had given him the stolen property. He said he took several steps back away from the suspect, and the male took off running toward Highway 63.

Reviewing the security cameras, I was able to physically see the suspect concealing several tools underneath his gray hoodie. I printed out a picture of the suspect we were looking for to show the other officers. A burnt-off copy of the security footage was placed into evidence.

During this time, another officer initiated a traffic stop on a suspicious vehicle circling the Lowe's parking lot. The driver, Dan, had a suspended driver's license and was placed under arrest. Further investigation revealed that Dan was waiting on his friend, Brandon, to exit Lowe's. Dan said he had no idea what had happened, but saw several police officers quickly arriving. He told us he knew his driver's license was suspended and had decided to leave the area but was pulled over.

I showed Dan a picture of the robbery suspect whom he identified as his friend, Brandon. Surprisingly, Dan said he could call Brandon and ask him where he was. Dan said Brandon was probably trying to contact him for a ride.

While in the booking room, Dan called Brandon and told him he was looking for him and to verify his location. Once Dan got off the phone, he told us Brandon said he was waiting for him at the baseball fields across from the movie theater.

I rushed to the area along with a state highway patrolman and a sheriff's deputy in front of me. When we were a block before the movie theater, the state highway patrol officer made a left turn on the road. Then the sheriff's deputy made a right turn on the road that ran up toward the park. So I continued straight toward the baseball fields.

I noticed a lot of parents with young children walking up the hill to the park for the annual Easter egg hunt. Realizing the event was getting ready to begin in a half hour, I knew we had to locate the robbery suspect.

As I looked around the area, I observed a male that resembled Brandon walking through the baseball field parking lot. He was wearing a white tank top instead of a gray hoodie. I parked my car along the street and approached the male. Before I reached him, Brandon glanced behind his left shoulder. With a startled expression, he quickly turned away and took off sprinting toward the field behind the baseball fields.

I radioed into dispatch that I was in foot pursuit of the suspect from the Lowe's robbery behind the park's baseball fields. Brandon had run between the parking lot and the ball fields and cut across a soccer field. As I chased behind him, I felt how heavy my ten-pound gun belt was and heard the loud clanging noise of my handcuffs.

Brandon then approached a chain-link fence located at the end of the soccer field and climbed over it. Shaking my head, I jogged around the fence to the other side. Surprisingly, I saw another police officer running toward us down a steep hill from the park. This gave me the burst of energy I needed to continue running after the suspect.

A male who was sitting along the sidewalk with his grandmother, waiting to watch the Easter egg hunt, saw me chasing the suspect. Without hesitation, the male grabbed his grandmother's hot pink walker and began shoving Brandon back. Miraculously, this stopped him from running any further. Unexpectedly, Brandon tripped and fell to the ground. The other officer and I were able to apprehend him and place him in handcuffs.

I searched Brandon and located two pocket knives in his front pocket. I also found two syringes there. One needle was completely filled with a clear liquid. Thankfully, both needles were securely capped. Otherwise, I could have been pricked by the needle. Brandon tried to say they were not his needles and he did not know how they got into his jeans.

As I transported Brandon to the county jail, he frantically began begging me to let him go. Brandon said he would give me information on who was selling heroin or meth. I informed him he could talk to our drug task force and they could try to contact the prosecutor's office.

While booking Brandon into jail, I asked him if the clear liquid inside the needle was going to test positive for heroin. Brandon looked at me with a disgusted facial expression and said, "No, it's meth." I placed the needle into evidence to be sent to the lab to verify that it contained methamphetamines. Brandon was still facing another felony charge for the possession of a controlled substance along with the first-degree robbery charge.

Unfortunately, in the back of every officer's mind, they are worried about their own safety and going home to their families. Every law enforcement officer takes extra precautions to make sure they do not come into physical contact with dangerous chemicals, narcotics, or blood. The last thing any patrolmen wants is to be stabbed by a used needle. Then they would have to go through several blood tests to verify that they had not been contaminated with a disease.

UGLINESS AND STRANGENESS

Occasionally, patrolmen will encounter peculiar, uncontrollable, and unexpected behavior and actions from others. Due to suspects' odd and bizarre actions, an officer might be left asking themselves what had happened and shaking their heads in disbelief. I experienced several incidents where an individual's strange behavior caught me off guard.

One incident was on a Sunday afternoon at four o'clock in July 2014. I heard an officer dispatched to attempt to locate a black female named Jade, age sixteen, who had run away from her foster home. Dispatch stated that the juvenile was wearing a black tee shirt and blue jeans and had her black hair pulled back in a ponytail. They informed us she was last seen on Tenth Street traveling westbound.

As I left the police department parking lot, I made a left turn onto Tenth Street to search the area. I passed a juvenile fitting the description walking on the sidewalk. She gave me a startled expression and turned away quickly.

I attempted to turn my car around, but I noticed in my rearview mirror that the female made a swift left turn toward the city hall parking lot. I made the left turn and saw Jade sprinting across the empty parking lot.

I radioed to the officer and dispatch, informing them the location of the runaway juvenile and that she was running from me. The patrolman stated he was en route to my direction.

As I raced across the empty parking lots, I observed Jade run behind a business. I exited my car and ordered the female to stop. Surprisingly she looked over her shoulder and slowed to a stop. I hastily approached Jade and placed her in handcuffs I detained her until the other officer arrived. She gave me no problems while we were waiting.

When the officer responded to our location, we placed Jade in the back seat of his patrol car to transport her back to her home. Abruptly she became irate and furious, yelling for us to "f**king let her go." Jade then laid across the back seats and began kicking the rear passenger window trying to break it out.

We secured Jade in her seat so she was unable to cause damage to the car. The officer transported her to the police department. While at the station we contacted the Division of Family Services to verify how they wanted to handle one of their runaway juveniles.

Jade was placed into a temporary holding cell. She deliberately began cussing and rattling the metal cell door. Jade then knelt down on the concrete floor and attempted to bang her head on it. We rushed into the cell to stop her from hurting herself. It took three officers to hold her down until ambulance personnel arrived.

Unfortunately, Jade continued to scream and yell at the top of her lungs. She looked at me menacingly and called me a "white cracker," then cursed me out using the c-word several times." Amusingly, these were new words I had never been called yet, and they were coming out of a sixteen-year-old's mouth. I was stunned; I could not believe how disrespectful Jade was and how much foul language she was using.

Within minutes, ambulance personnel arrived at the department with a stretcher. We began to secure Jade to it using soft restraints and buckles so she could be transported to the hospital. She attempted to claw and scratch us with her long fingernails while trying to undo the buckles. Finally, securing Jade to the stretcher, the ambulance crew were able to take her.

While at the hospital, Jade continued to be rude and disruptive by screaming and cussing. She even called a black male hospital employee the n-word. I was outraged by her demeanor and language.

I told her to watch her mouth and be respectful to all the employees. I informed Jade how they were there to help her and she needed to change her attitude. Jade just rolled her eyes.

We then secured her to the bed using soft restraints. Unexpectedly, Jade spit on the officer standing next to me. I didn't realize it, but some spit had gotten on my uniform sleeve. The emergency room nurses placed a spit mask on Jade, but she deliberately chewed through it, so another one had to be placed on her. I was astonished! I had not witnessed a female juvenile so rude, disrespectful, and disgusting to everyone trying to help her.

Tire Slasher

A cold November morning, at approximately at three o'clock, I responded to a gas station for a report of a stealing. As I pulled into the station, I located the victim, a taxicab driver, Luke, parked near the front of the business. The driver informed me that the intoxicated male, Tim, was picked up from a local bar and refused to pay his $3.50 fare. Luke said Tim was becoming arrogant and disgruntled, so he called the police.

I talked to Tim, who was sitting in the backseat. I informed him if he paid the $3.50, he would be allowed to go home. Tim said he did not have any money and he had no friends to call. I asked him why he called a taxicab service if he knew he was not able to pay. Tim sluggishly said he just wanted a ride home.

Luke stated he wanted to file charges against the male for stealing. Unbelievably, I had to arrest someone for failing to pay for a $3.50 service charge. Tim stepped out of the taxi, and I placed him under arrest. I transported him to the police department. I informed Tim he was going to be released on a ticket, but he would have a court date to appear for the stealing.

After the booking process, I asked Tim if there was anyone I could call for him to get a ride home. Tim rudely stated, "No, that's why I took a cab." Tim was released to go but became agitated that I was not willing to give him a ride home. He even had the audacity to ask me to call a cab for him. When he realized I was not going to call a taxi for him, he stormed out the front doors of the department. I thought that would be the last encounter with Tim for the night. Unfortunately, I was terribly mistaken.

An hour later, a dispatcher went out to his vehicle parked in the police parking lot near the front entrance door. He discovered his rear passenger side tire had been slashed with a knife. The dispatcher noticed that two other patrol cars that were parked there also had flat tires that appeared to be slashed.

I reviewed the security cameras to the department parking lot, and they showed my arrest suspect exiting the front doors. Tim walked past the dispatcher's blue Blazer and suddenly stopped and began looking around. Thinking this was odd, I watched as Tim squatted down by the Blazer's rear passenger side tire. It appeared he had something in his right hand. Tim then turned to the patrol car parked next to the Blazer and stabbed its rear driver's side tire. Looking around, he got up, walked down toward the end of the parking lot, and bent down by another patrol car's rear tire. Tim showed no remorse for his actions and casually left the area as if he did nothing wrong.

What nerve! I could not believe Tim had the audacity to vandalize patrol vehicles in the department parking lot! I knew what I was going to do. I arrived at Tim's residence and arrested him again two hours later for destruction of property. Tim was now transported to the county jail for a twenty-four-hour hold, pending warrants. Sadly, this all began because an intoxicated male refused to pay $3.50 for cab fare.

Odd Behavior

On a Wednesday morning in May, at ten o'clock, I was dispatched to check the well-being of a four-feet-eleven, 150-pound female aged fifty-five. I was informed the female could be heard talking loudly and that a lot of banging noises were coming from her apartment.

I arrived at the downstairs apartment and contacted the female, Jeanette. After talking to her, she appeared to be all right and did not seem to need any help. Jeanette then unexpectedly asked me, "Do you think I should ask them if the baby is hungry? I was confused because I did not see anyone else in the apartment." Still, I said, "Okay."

Jeanette then turned to the vacant couch and asked an imaginary person if the baby was hungry. I just stood there in bewilderment. I had never witnessed someone holding a conversation with no one there. One minute she was perfectly fine, and the next minute she was talking nonsense. Unfortunately, no officer is trained in how to handle this behavior.

Jeanette then told me in a serious tone that they would not get out of her house. I asked her who "they" were. I wondered if she had someone in her back bedroom. She said people were living in her vents, and she showed me where she had Maced her vents.

I told Jeanette I would search her apartment and get out anyone who was in it. I did a quick walk-through, knowing I would not see anyone. I radioed in to dispatch to have the paramedics respond to my location. I was unable to determine what exactly was going on with Jeanette.

Before the ambulance arrived, I asked Jeanette to show me her prescriptions. This way, I could advise the paramedics of what she was taking and, maybe, know if she was mixing the wrong prescriptions together.

Jeanette stated that all her prescriptions were in her purse. She then would change the topic to how she was thirsty and needed a drink of Gatorade. I had to ask her several times to hand me her purse.

When the paramedics arrived at Jeanette's residence, she started to look for her purse again. I observed it sitting on the kitchen table. Suddenly, Jeanette said, "Oh, I know! My purse is behind the couch." The next thing I know, she was down on her hands and knees trying to squeeze behind her couch. Jeanette began yelling, "You get out of there! Get out of there!"

I pulled Jeanette from behind the couch and told her there was no one there. I thought she was going to calm down for the paramedics on the scene, but instead she pulled away from me. Before I could grab her, Jeanette quickly hopped headfirst behind her sectional couch. With only her behind and two short legs kicking in the air, I almost started laughing. I had never seen someone get stuck headfirst behind a couch. I knew this was not normal behavior, but I had no clue what prescriptions would cause these abnormal behaviors.

Subsequently, the paramedic and I had to pull Jeanette up and over the couch by her legs. I informed them I had no idea why she was acting so oddly and that this was not Jeanette's normal behavior. She was loaded into the ambulance and transported to the hospital for evaluation. I informed her I would make sure no one was in her apartment and that she was safe.

Change of Mind

One Sunday afternoon in March, around 1:00 p.m., I was working my part-time job as a security officer in the hospital. I had two hours before the next security officer arrived to work. I got radioed to respond to the emergency room for an unruly suicidal male patient.

As I entered the emergency room, the nurses told me a black male, named Roy, age forty-eight, was causing a loud disturbance from his secure room. They informed me Roy had checked himself into the hospital, admitting he had suicidal thoughts. He was being held for an evaluation. Only now he decided that he no longer wanted help and wanted to leave the hospital. The nurses advised Roy that since he made comments about harming himself, they could not allow him to leave without being evaluated.

When I walked over to the secure room, I heard Roy yelling through the closed door and saying how they could not keep him here. I informed him he needed to stop yelling and disturbing the other patients. Roy told me he was being held against his will and he wanted to leave.

I informed Roy that since he had made a comment about wanting to harm himself, he had to wait for a physician to evaluate him. When the doctor cleared him, he would be allowed to leave. Roy stated he had been waiting for several hours for a doctor to talk to him, and no one had spoken to him.

Roy angrily looked at me and said he no longer needed help and he was ready to leave. I told him that was not an option at this time. Then Roy said he needed to use the restroom. I allowed him to use the bathroom while I waited outside the door for him.

When he exited the restroom, he looked straight at me and said, "I'm not going back in that room. You will just have to arrest me." I told him to place his hands behind his back. Shockingly, Roy complied and placed both of his hands behind his back. Holding his hands together, I walked him near his room. Then I opened the door and pushed him into the room and secured the door.

Roy became furious! He was cussing and kicking the door! Roy said, "You better f——king let me go." I told him to watch his mouth and he did not need to be using foul language.

During this time, the nurses came over to Roy's room. We were able to secure him to the bed in soft restraints. Afterward, Roy became calm and relaxed. Thankfully, we had no further incidents with him causing a noisy, disruptive scene.

Technically, I had no grounds to place Roy under arrest. Plus, the jail would not hold him without a "fit for confinement" form. The form would have to come from the hospital and be signed by a physician since he had made a suicidal comment.

Traffic Stop

Another female officer I worked with initiated a traffic stop in the late evening. As she walked up to the driver's side window, she heard a loud knocking coming from the trunk. When she asked the driver what he had in the trunk, he gave her a startled facial expression and said, "Nothing."

She then called for another officer to assist her on her traffic stop since the vehicle had five individuals inside the car. When the other officer arrived at her location, she had everyone exit the vehicle. She then had the driver unlock his trunk to verify that nothing was in it.

As the driver opened the trunk, an intoxicated twenty-two-year-old three-feet-five little person with blond hair named Jamie popped up. She had her arms straight in the air and said, "Here I am." The officer stepped back for a moment because she had no idea a person was going to jump up at her.

The female officer told Jamie she needed to get out of the trunk. She then asked Jamie if she needed help down. Jamie nodded her head. The officer went to pick up Jamie. All of a sudden, Jamie started rapidly kicking both of her legs in the air, trying to kick the officer. She started yelling and cursing, "Put me down! Put me down!"

We were familiar with the female because every encounter an officer had had with her was for intoxication. The driver was informed he was not allowed to have anyone ride in the trunk and everyone had to be properly buckled up in a seat belt.

All law enforcement officers remember the encounters they have with individuals whose behavior is strange, odd, ugly, and bizarre. Unfortunately, every situation is different, and there are no set solutions for an individual's bizarre actions.

OFFICER NEEDING ASSISTANCE

No one in law enforcement wants to hear an officer calling for assistance. Listening to another officer out of breath saying they need more officers now is heart stopping. You feel like you cannot get to them fast enough. Automatically, your mind visualizes the worst-case scenario.

That's precisely what happened on a Thursday night, around ten o'clock, while I was cruising around. I heard my corporal call out a traffic stop at a gas station on Highway 72 at the southeastern side of town. He was known for making a lot of drug arrests.

I began to head to that direction just to make sure he was secure. Next thing I heard over my car radio was my corporal saying he needed immediate assistance. Then the radio went silent. Suddenly, he broke the eerie silence by saying to have them expedite.

For a brief moment my heart skipped a beat and I had to make myself take a breath. Then my adrenaline kicked in full blast. As I activated my lights and sirens I accelerated to the gas station. Thankfully, I was less than four blocks away but it felt like my car could not get there fast enough.

Never does a patrolman want to hear an officer call for help. In a split second, you are filled with dread because you don't want any harm to come to a fellow patrolman. Then at the same moment, you experience a burst of rage and anger toward anyone who wants to harm you or any other law enforcement.

I arrived at the gas station and pulled into the parking lot. I saw my Corporal wrestling around with a tall slender male in his mid-twenties, on the right side of the building. I slammed my vehicle in park and rushed out to assist the officer. I noticed my Corporal was attempting to take Brian to the ground so he could secure him in handcuffs. However, Brian remained on his feet and kept pulling his arms away. I approached him with my Taser in hand. I had every intention of deploying it on the suspect if he continued to resist arrest.

A Taser is a handheld weapon that fires two metal barb fish-hooks attached to wires, causing temporary incapacitation of an individual for five seconds during every trigger pull. As police officers, we are trained to use a Taser for nonlethal force, and it is the same level of force as Mace or pepper spray.

The suspect grabbed hold of my Taser, cupping it with both his hands and pulling it toward his stomach. At the exact same moment, my corporal grabbed Brian's arm and flung him over his shoulder to the ground. Brian kept hold of my Taser as he flew to the ground, ripping it completely out of my hands.

I suddenly realized that if Brian turned the Taser toward us, he could incapacitate us and take our guns to use against us. Then I was contemplating how I would stop him and if I needed to use deadly force.

Brian was on the ground, but he had the audacity to have both arms underneath his chest. The corporal commanded him to place both arms behind his back, but he continued to refuse. I was attempting to get Brian's left arm from underneath him when I noticed, in the corner of my eye, another male rushing over to us. I yelled for him to get back. The startled male stopped in place and said, "Jess, it's me."

As I looked at the younger male, I realized he was an employee who worked in the emergency department at the hospital. I told him to grab an arm. With the male's assistance, we were able to secure Brian in handcuffs.

I later discovered that Brian was under the influence of meth-amphetamines. He also had two small clear baggies containing a white powder concealed in his front jean pockets. The white powder tested positive for methamphetamines. We ran Brian's information and discovered that he had an active warrant for possession of narcotics. While at the jail, Brian confessed that the reason he was resisting was because he did not want to go back to jail.

Thankfully, everyone went home alive that night because Brian had his mind set to get away by any means necessary. Looking back, I realize it was a blessing that the citizen saw us and rushed to our aid; otherwise, the suspect could have used deadly force.

Always on Duty

On a Friday night at midnight, the other shift's sergeant, my boyfriend who was later to become my husband, had just finished a twelve-hour shift and was heading home. He was approximately five blocks from the residence when he observed a seventeen-year-old male pulling a metal stop signpost out of the ground.

The seventeen-year-old male noticed the patrol car traveling toward his direction and froze in place for a brief moment. He then threw the stop sign on the ground and took off running toward the elementary school. The sergeant slammed the car in park and chased the suspect. While at the station, we heard the sergeant broadcast he was in a foot pursuit near Mark Twain Elementary School. The sergeant stated he needed another unit to come to his location.

I never heard him ask for assistance, so this made my heart fill with dread and uneasiness. Taking a breath, I ran to my patrol car and hastily turned on my lights and sirens. As I accelerated to his location, I felt like I could not get there fast enough. I just kept saying out loud, "Someone get to him now" over and over again.

Amazingly, another officer was able to respond quicker than me. The sergeant had apprehended the seventeen-year-old and already had him placed in handcuffs.

This incident helped me recognize that as an officer, we are never technically off work, even after a long twelve-hour shift. Patrolmen have a duty to report any crimes they witness. Most officers will feel obligated to help anyone in need. Even when officers are off the clock, they are still keeping their eyes and ears open for anyone who is breaking the law. Definitely, if an officer needs assistance, every officer on duty will respond if able.

Unfortunately, law enforcement is a dangerous profession. Sadly, certain criminals come only to steal, kill, and destroy. They will also do anything to keep themselves out of prison, even taking the life of another.

In 2015, there were 124 law enforcement officers killed nationwide in the line of duty. Forty-two officers were shot and killed, fifty-two died from traffic incidents, and thirty died from other causes.

THREE IN THE AFTERNOON

On Friday, July 11, 2014, at 3:00 p.m., I was just beginning my shift. Without warning, a loud alarm sounded on my portable radio. Dispatch advised that a distraught female had barricaded herself in her bedroom with a large hunting knife. I rushed out of the police department with several other officers and responded to the female's residence.

As I arrived, she was speaking foul, crude curse words. In Psalm 34:13, it says, "Keep your tongue from evil and your lips from telling lies." James 3:9 says, "With the tongue we praise our Lord and Father and with it we curse human beings who have been made in God's likeness. Out of the same mouth praise and cursing. My brothers and sisters, this should not be." At the female's home, I contacted a male, identified as Jim, who was the female's husband. Jim informed me that Barb had been very depressed for the last two weeks. He stated she refused to take her antidepressant medication, and he was extremely concerned about her. Jim said Barb made a comment a few minutes ago that she was just going to end it all. Then she walked into the bedroom carrying his large hunting knife. He told us he tried to get into the bedroom, but she had pushed something against the door so he was unable to enter the room. Jim said that this was when he called the police.

At this time, an officer knocked on the bedroom door. What did Barb do? She knocked back. I laughed to myself because this was the first time I witnessed this type of odd action. The officer announced, "Police department" and told her she needed to come out of the room.

Barb yelled back that she was fine and we all needed to go away. The officer informed Barb we needed to check on her and verify she was secure. He told her if she would step out into the living room and talk to us, we would be able to leave her residence a lot sooner.

Barb refused to open the door. Suddenly, we could hear another large piece of furniture being scooted across the floor toward the bedroom door. The officer tried to push open the door, but it would not open.

The sergeant spoke to another SWAT (Special Weapons and Tactics) team member, advising a plan to safely get into the bedroom and secure the female from harming herself. The sergeant said that an officer standing outside would break the bedroom window and toss in a can of Mace. The sergeant then turned to me and asked if I would go assist the other officer on taking calls on the road.

As I walked out to my patrol car, I wished I could remain at this barricade situation. I heard the other road officer call out that he was in a foot pursuit with a male suspect across town.

I raced across town with my lights and sirens blazing. I located the patrolman standing in the middle of the road. Exhausted, he stated that he had lost sight of the skinny male in his early twenties wearing a white tee shirt and tan cargo shorts. The officer explained how he had initiated a traffic stop on a vehicle a couple of blocks from this location. He said the suspect, Austin, had exited out the front passenger door and took off running in between houses and into the wooded area. The officer said he chased Austin but had lost sight of him.

I drove the officer two blocks back to his patrol car, and we began canvassing the area. The other officer walked the wood line where Austin was last seen running. A small black pistol was located lying on the ground right before the woods.

Suddenly, our dispatcher radioed that an unknown male had run into a residence, only four blocks from our location, took off his tee shirt and told them not to call the police. The suspect then exited the residence in an unknown direction.

As we arrived at that residence, the homeowner, Deborah, stated that she had left her front door open to let in some fresh air. She said an unknown male in his early twenties had opened her screen door and rushed into her home. Deborah said that at first she thought it was her son coming inside. Frantically, the male told her not to call the cops, and he took off his shirt and turned it inside out. She told us that he then exited out the front door, running away in an unknown direction. Deborah stated she had never seen him before and figured she better call the police due to his odd behavior.

The other officer continued to circle around the residence on top of the hill, attempting to locate the suspect. I drove around the bottom of the hill, which was a dead-end road surrounded by homes. I then exited my vehicle and began walking along the wood line.

Immediately, I heard loud shouting at the top of the hill. The officer was yelling at someone to drop the knife. Unable to see anything but trees, I located a clearing in the woods on the far-right side and started climbing up the steep hill. I said to myself, "I'm coming, boys." Then I heard the officer yell, "He's going back down! He's going back down!"

Looking up, I saw the suspect, Austin, with no shirt, dive down the rocky, wooded hill. He got back on his feet and continued running down the hill toward me. I rushed back down the hill and quickly ran along the wood line to the location where Austin was running. As he exited the woods into the clearing, I deployed my Taser, and one probe struck Austin in the chest. Unfortunately, I was unable to observe if the second probe had struck him.

Austin stopped where he was. His entire body locked up, and he fell over on his right side in a fetal position. Shockingly, Austin was still clutching an open two-inch pocket knife in his right hand. I was furious when I realized he had been running downhill toward me with an open knife.

I demanded that he drop the knife. He did not comply, so I instantly stunned him with the Taser in the back of the leg. It was unclear if the second probe was contacting the suspect's skin. For complete incapacitation of someone, both metal probes have to contact the body with at least an eight-inch space between probes; otherwise, the individual can feel pain but will still fight through it.

During the rush of excitement, I forgot to remove my finger off the trigger. So the Taser was going to continue releasing 50,000 volts until I stopped pressing the trigger.

I automatically let go of the trigger, and Austin quickly tossed the knife and rolled onto his stomach with both hands behind his back. I didn't think he wanted to be Tased again.

Austin was placed into handcuffs. The officer came running down from the top of the hill after the suspect. I was relieved I did not have to shoot the suspect because I would have had no idea that the patrolman was chasing right behind him. That could have turned into an even more dangerous and deadly situation.

Once handcuffed, Austin began crying that his "balls were on fire." He then had the audacity to ask me for something to drink. I scornfully told Austin why he should never run from the police. I emphasized that when an officer tells him to stop, he better listen.

During this time, I informed dispatch I had one in custody and he had been Tased. Running Austin's information through central communications, I was advised he had a nonextraditable warrant from Arkansas. This meant that no law enforcement from Arkansas was going to drive to Missouri to pick him up. So we had no grounds to hold him for the Arkansas warrant. Austin heard the information and could not believe he had run for no reason. Now we had charges filed against him for fleeing from a police officer and unlawfully entering a residence.

I later discovered that while I was apprehending Austin, the other police officers had made entrance into the suicidal female's bedroom and deployed their Taser on her. Unfortunately, our dispatcher was confused and thought I was still at the barricade with the suicidal female suspect.

Subsequently when Austin was transported to the hospital, other officers were escorting Barb, the disgruntled female, to the same location for evaluation. While Austin was waiting in the emergency room, he was telling the transporting officer that the little five-foot blond officer can punch hard. When the patrolman told me this,

I had to laugh. First, I am almost five feet five and I never struck him; only my Taser did.

While standing outside in the ambulance bay in front of the emergency doors, a nurse approached me. She advised that the hospital had no grounds to hold Barb for a psychotic evaluation since she was not making any comments or threats to harm herself or others. I informed her of the events we just encountered with Barb barricading herself in her room with a hunting knife. The nurse stated she understood our concerns, but by their rules and regulations, they could not keep her at the hospital. Unbelievably, I just shook my head.

Barb then walked right past the emergency exit doors trying to escape. As I went back into the hospital, I observed four individuals carrying Barb back to her room as she continued to kick, swing, and squirm.

Unfortunately, to protect Barb and others, we placed her under arrest on a temporary hold until her husband, Jim, could receive the proper ninety-six-hour hold commit order paperwork signed by a judge. Then Barb would be held in the hospital for the remainder of her evaluation.

Once Austin was completed with his physical examination, he was released back into our custody to be transported to the jail. I was informed that only one probe had made contact in his skin, and when he jumped down the hill, his testicle struck a rock. Shaking my head, I knew I would never forget the first suspect I had to Tase.

Amazingly, this chaotic afternoon began at 3:00 p.m., and we had two individuals Tased before 5:00 p.m.

TROUBLESOME TIMES

Growing up, I heard the saying "When one door closes, another one opens." But when you have to live through it, how do you act or respond?

My world turned upside down in January 2015, and it felt like a door had slammed shut. My fiancé, David, and I arrived back to work at the police department after a week's vacation. This was our fourth Christmas we had spent together at his parents' residence in West Virginia.

Unforeseen events transpired the week we were off work. We returned back to the department to learn that we could no longer work on the same shift together even though for the six months prior to our vacation we had worked side by side on the same shift. I was furious because we had never caused a problem nor had a complaint brought against us. We were always professional and kept home life separate from work.

We felt like we both were being punished for no apparent reason. No one even considered to mention the shift change to us. The police department just waited till we returned to observe our new work schedule.

I honestly had quit my job that day and several times afterward in my mind. So I kept working, but continued to look for any new job opportunity.

Unfortunately, that exact week, I discovered through an e-mail that I had gotten passed up for a corporal's position by another police officer with less years of experience. I felt devastated, hurt, and aggravated all at the same time.

To top off my frustration, my fiancé and I were scheduled to work on separate shifts with no days off together. Unfortunately, this was our set work schedule for the next six months. I could not understand why it felt like the rug had been pulled out from under us and all doors were slamming shut. I had no inkling that God was ordaining my footsteps and had greater plans in store for the both of us.

Back in January 2015, I had recorded my feelings in a journal to assist me in coping with these rough circumstances. I had actually written down that I hoped no other employee got treated the way we did. I told myself, "Head up! I know God has a purpose for me. I'll keep my eyes and ears open for opportunities. I knew this was a character builder, and God wanted me to be like his son, Jesus." I also wrote how I hoped I was doing a good job, but it was hard and it hurt. I recognized how my thoughts were extremely negative at this time. Then I wrote, "This too shall pass. Don't worry. Be happy."

It's hard to believe that I wrote this because I had never gone to church and had never read the Bible, but I had always believed in God. I just knew in my heart everything would work out for a reason, even when I did not know what that reason was.

In February, we started considering the idea of looking at law enforcement jobs in West Virginia, where my fiancé's family lived. We put our application in at a police department and sheriff department. The police department was hiring two police officers. We completed their written civil service test and ranked in the top five applicants. I was informed that my fiancé scored in second place and I came in fourth place. Regrettably, they informed us we would have to come back to West Virginia in a couple of weeks for an interview.

We were determined, so we made the ten-hour drive back to West Virginia the next month for our interviews. Unfortunately, the staff at the police department was unprepared for the interview. They were reading my application when I was sitting in front of them.

We returned home not feeling confident or reassured in the interviews and later discovered the department had actually hired the male that scored the highest on the written test. They also hired a female, who was a friend of theirs, who had scored below me and who was not a certified police officer. This was a major blow, and all I could do was keep looking for another job opportunity that came my way.

In May 2015, David and I left for West Virginia again to take another written civil service and physical test. We both had applied for a deputy position at a sheriff's department near his hometown.

During the physical test, we both had to see how many push-ups and sit-ups we could do in a minute. Then we had to run a mile and a half in ninety-degree weather on a black asphalt track. We both passed the physical tests but had to wait to see what our scores were on the written part.

Remarkably a week later, we got an e-mail stating we both passed our written test. David scored eleventh place, and I had tied with three others for the twenty-fifth place out of sixty applicants. The e-mail advised they were only hiring three deputies and they would be looking at the top ten applicants. Unfortunately, the rest of us were on their waiting list, which would be good for two years.

Feeling defeated, discouraged, and conquered, we realized we needed to figure out if we wanted to stay in the police department where we were working or find another job. Sadly, I realized, to have days off with my fiancé, I would have to find another job. I chose to put my application into the local sheriff's department.

In June 2015, I applied at the sheriff's department. I had to complete another physical test. I passed all their requirements and was the second runner-up for the deputy position. I was informed at this time they were looking at the first runner-up and only had one position to fill. I thanked them for the opportunity and went home with another disappointment under my belt.

I truly could not understand how our life had been turned upside down for no apparent reason. Prior to leaving for our Christmas vacation, life was going great. We had worked on the same shift rotation for six months with the exact same days off together. But now we had not even one day off together for six months and the only time we saw each other was when one of us was leaving work and the other was clocking on.

Suddenly, our life began taking steps toward major changes. A couple of weeks later, I received a call from our local sheriff department stating that the deputy position was mine if I was still interested. I immediately accepted the position, and the next month, I started my new career as a deputy.

God is amazing! He knows when we are comfortable or set in our ways. We are more willing not to move or jump. God already knows He has to shake us up or slam a door shut to get us to realize that a better opportunity awaits us and to move on. I'm so thankful that He cares and loves us that much. We just always have to keep our eyes and ears open.

DEPUTY SHERIFF FOR A MONTH

In July 2015, I got hired as a deputy sheriff for Phelps County, Missouri. It was similar to my job as a patrolman for the city. The only differences were that I now wore a brown uniform instead of a dark navy blue, and I had to patrol and respond to calls to the entire county. Unfortunately, as a deputy, that meant if you needed another officer to respond, it could take a few minutes for them to reach your location.

My first emergency call was an unresponsive female who had apparently overdosed on heroin. I raced with lights and sirens blaring from the northern part of the county onto Interstate 44, to get to the far eastern side. Normally, it would take me five minutes or less to respond to all our calls in the city. It did take longer responding to certain portions of the county.

I arrived at the residence and located a female, Lindsey, lying on the living room floor breathing, but still unresponsive. Ambulance personnel had arrived at the same time, and they began to do sternum rubs on her.

Lindsey was drowsy but opened her eyes and began talking to us. Unbelievably, she was able to answer all the paramedics' questions, and her vitals checked out normal. We informed Lindsey that it would be an excellent idea to get checked out at the hospital, but she refused any medical treatment.

Her boyfriend, Steven, was with her and became agitated when she refused any further treatment. I informed them that we could not force her to seek treatment unless anything appeared to be life-threatening, but we highly recommended it. As we left the residence, we informed Lindsey to call us if she changed her mind or needed anything. She thanked us but still refused any other help.

Approximately thirty minutes later, dispatch sent us back to the same address for another call. This time it was for a physical domestic that was occurring between the female and her boyfriend.

Upon arrival, I located Lindsey walking down the long gravel driveway toward the main highway. She stated that after we had left, Steven's anger had intensified because she refused to go to the hospital. Lindsey said he began yelling at her and then slapped her in the face, calling her stupid. She told me Steven had finally driven off when she screamed at him that she was calling the police.

Lindsey's face was slightly red on both sides where she indicated Steven had slapped her. She stated she was leaving for the night and going to stay at a friend's house. She continued to refuse any medical treatment and stated she wanted to file charges against her boyfriend.

We searched the area for Steven, but were unable to locate him or his vehicle. As long as both individuals were separated for the night, then I knew no more physical altercations would occur.

Traffic Stop

After my second week as a deputy, I was cruising on Highway 63 through Rolla about to exit the city limits. I observed an older pickup truck traveling directly in front of me with its rear brake light not operating.

I quickly activated my lights and siren and initiated a traffic stop. The truck slowly pulled into a parking lot located along the right side of the highway. I cautiously approached the truck. I observed a male driver, identified as Gary, and a female passenger, identified as Margaret.

I informed Gary that the reason for the stop was due to his rear brake light not operating. I did recognize Gary from previous traffic stops and recalled I had written him a seat belt ticket when I was a city police officer.

Gary and Margaret were very polite, and I was just going to release them on a verbal warning for the vehicle equipment. But when I ran both profiles through central communications, I was informed they both had an active warrant for failing to appear in court on an original charge of a seat belt violation.

Consequently, the ten-dollar seat belt ticket was now a fifty-dollar cash-only bond warrant with a mandatory court date appearance. I had to place both Gary and Margaret under arrest and transported them to the county jail.

I did wonder if Gary realized I was the officer that had cut him a break before on his speeding but wrote him a ticket for the seat belt violation. Both the driver and his wife remained courteous even though they were not thrilled about being arrested on their active warrants.

Bizarre Kidnapping

It was 11:00 p.m. on a Friday night, and I was dispatched to a county road to attempt to locate and check the well-being of an eighteen-year-old female named Hannah. The reporting party was identified as the girl's mother, Cindy. She said she had not heard back from her daughter for five hours and was getting worried about her.

Cindy informed me that Hannah had recently moved in with her twenty-year-old boyfriend, Tony, but they had problems. She said Hannah was not happy with Tony and had mentioned how he seemed to be trying to control her. Cindy said Hannah was supposed to retrieve a few of her personal belongings five hours ago from Tony's apartment and to come back to her house. She said she had not seen nor heard from her. Cindy said she tried calling and sending her daughter text messages, but still had not received any response. She stated she was getting more frightened about Hannah's safety. Cindy informed me she had driven by Tony's apartment to locate Hannah, but there was no answer and her vehicle was gone. She said she thought she had to wait twenty-four hours to file a missing-person report, but she could not wait that long.

I informed Cindy she did not have to wait twenty-four hours to file a report and we would attempt to locate her daughter. Doing a trace on Hannah's cell phone, it pinged on a county road surrounded by woods. I responded to the location and drove down several gravel roads looking for their vehicle or anyone in the area.

I observed a four-door black car parked on a small gravel road near a wooded area. The lights were off, and I approached the vehicle with another deputy.

As I looked inside the vehicle, I noticed a male in his twenties sitting in the driver's seat and a female in the front passenger seat. They were both slumped back in their seats asleep. Tapping on the passenger's side window, I informed them that I was with the sheriff's department and to open the doors.

The startled female woke up and slowly unlocked the passenger's side door. I recognized her as Hannah, whom we were attempting to locate. I had Hannah step out of the vehicle and walk toward the back of the car. She complied.

I asked Hannah what they were doing out in the middle of nowhere this late at night. At first, she denied anything was wrong. Hannah said they were just stopped for the night and fell asleep in their vehicle.

I told Hannah that her mother had sent us to check on her because she had not called or texted her back. Hannah began shaking, and her eyes began to water. She said her boyfriend, Tony, discovered tonight that she was going to leave him and move back home with her mother. Hannah said Tony became angry and told her that she wasn't going to leave him.

Hannah told me that Tony took her cell phone away from her so she could not call anyone and he had it on him now. She said he had also grabbed her car keys from her and drove her to this secluded area, thinking no one would find them. Hannah said she had no idea where they were or how to get home. She had no idea where Tony planned on taking her in the morning. She told me Tony was controlling in the past, but not to this extreme.

The other deputy was talking to Tony who admitted to having Hannah's cell phone in his rear back pocket. He denied keeping her in the wooded area against her will. Tony tried to explain how Hannah was free to go at any time.

Tony was placed under arrest for kidnapping. Hannah was given back her cell phone and car keys. I informed her to call her mom and let her know she was all right. I made sure Hannah was in good condition to drive and told her to follow us out of the area to the main road. I then called Cindy to inform her Hannah was safe and on her way home. We had Tony in custody. Cindy could not thank us enough for finding her daughter and bringing her home safely.

Physical Domestic

Another deputy and I responded to a county road at 6:30 p.m. We were attempting to locate a female, Barb, and check her well-being. The reporting party was Barb's son, who had informed us that her new husband, Mike, was known to get physically abusive with her in the past. Her son stated he was unable to contact her by phone and just wanted to make sure she was not in any danger.

Unfortunately, Barb's son did not know her exact address, but gave us a description of the house and her gray car. I arrived on the county road and remarkably located a residence that fit the description. To verify if it was the correct address, I ran the vehicle's plate through dispatch. The license plate came back registered to the female we were trying to locate.

I knocked on the front door, and a female, identified as Barb, answered the door. I asked her if everything was all right because her son was unable to reach her on her cell phone. Barb said her cell phone battery must have died without her knowledge.

I asked her if her husband was also home. Barb said in a shaky voice that her husband, Mike, was asleep on the couch. She asked if we could please let him know that she did not call the police.

I told her we would make sure that Mike understood that we were there to make sure both of them were all right and that she did not call us. Before I entered the house, I asked Barb, "Do you feel safe with your husband?"

Barb looked away and said, "Of course."

I shook my head because I automatically knew she was afraid Mike was going to take his anger out on her. But Barb refused to mention anything or ask us for help.

As I entered the living room, I observed a male, identified as Mike, passed out on the couch, snoring. There were several empty beer bottles scattered on the floor. I awakened Mike, and we identified ourselves as sheriff deputies. I told him we were there just to make sure they were both all right and that no one had received any physical injuries. Mike slowly woke up. He became furious when he discovered that officers were in his home and demanded to know who called us.

I informed Mike we just had a call to check on them both, but that his wife had not called us. I told him we just wanted to make sure they both were safe and secure. Mike was becoming ruder and more upset that we were there.

After verifying that no one was injured or needed our assistance, we left. Barb walked us to the front door, and I advised her to call her son just to let him know she was all right. I asked Barb again if she felt secure with her husband.

Barb said, "Of course," and apologized for us having to come to their house. As we left the residence, I had an urge to do more to help Barb, but when she denied needing any help, there was nothing legally we could do.

Approximately an hour later, we received a call from dispatch that a physical domestic had just occurred. The reporting party located a blond female in her late forties walking on a county road with a fresh black eye, bloody nose, and a fresh cut on her lower lip. He drove the female to a local gas station near Interstate 44 and called the police.

Upon arrival, I immediately recognized the female victim as Barb. With one look at her battered and bloody face, I felt so much anger, rage, and disgust toward any man that could lay a fist or hand on a female.

Barb saw me and began weeping. She said, "Mike did not know what he was doing." Barb continued to say how Mike had had a rough day at work, and when the police showed up at their house, his anger took over.

Barb did finally admit that Mike punched her several times in the face with a closed fist. She told me that when she tried to leave the house, Mike held her right arm and slammed the screen door shut on it. Barb said he continued to cuss at her the entire time. Barb said she was able to pull her arm out of Mike's grasp and took off running from their residence. She told me she began walking on the county road to get away, when a kind individual gave her a ride to the gas station.

I told Barb that Mike had no reason or excuse to lay a hand on her no matter how bad of a day he had.

During this time, ambulance personnel arrived on the scene and gave Barb ice for her wounds. Barb continued to refuse any medical treatment, saying she was fine and she was not going to the hospital. Barb said she would spend the night at a friend's residence and not return home for the night.

I told Barb, "We were going to go arrest Mike for the physical assault." Barb began crying again, saying, "She did not want Mike to get arrested."

I told Barb she needed to think about taking care of herself and that she did not deserve to be hit by anyone, especially her husband. I informed Barb that she could go to the courthouse in the morning and get a restraining order filed against her husband. A restraining order is a court order stating the suspect would have to stay away from the victim and their residence until a court hearing was scheduled. Then if her husband tried to violate the restraining order by contacting her in any way, he would be automatically arrested.

Barb nodded her head that she understood, but I knew in my heart she was not going to do anything against her husband or to change her circumstances.

I responded with another deputy back to Barb's residence to locate her husband, Mike. As I pulled up to the house, Mike stormed out of the front door with no shirt, yelling and demanding we stay off his property.

I told Mike we were there because of the physical altercation that had occurred between him and his wife. Mike looked at me and said, "The b——h deserved it." Then he gave me a smug grin.

I made Mike turn around with his hands behind his back. Mike turned around but continued to pull his arms away. The other deputy grabbed his right arm, and I grabbed his left and we were able to secure him safely in handcuffs. Mike became even more irate and cussed me out the entire ride back to the jail. As I drove, I had to listen to Mike tell me how deputies think they are tough because they have a gun and badge.

Prior to arriving at the jail, I had our dispatch inform the jailers that we were arriving with an intoxicated male who was becoming more uncooperative. As I pulled into the jail garage, several jailers were waiting for us and escorted Mike to his own cell until he could sober up.

Unfortunately, this was not the first physical altercation I witnessed where the female victim will blame herself and believe she deserved what she received. The female victim will then lie, deny, and beg the police not to arrest the male suspect. Sadly, the female lives through so much emotional abuse daily that she truly believes she is the cause of all their problems and that she's worthless. This is not true. It's an unhealthy relationship.

As a police officer, I try to help victims by giving them information to keep them safe and to get them away from their abusive situation. It is ultimately their choice to ask for help and to take the steps needed to change their dangerous lifestyles.

LED BY FAITH

When a door closes, God will always open a window. You just have to have faith and be patient with your eyes and ears open. I learned this from experience. I had no clue what God had in store for me and my family; but He had big plans for us. All I had to do was take the first step toward Him, and He took care of everything else. God is amazing!

The same month I started my job as a deputy, my fiancé, David, received a call from the county sheriff department in West Virginia. They informed him they were hiring for a deputy position and asked him if he could come in for an interview and polygraph.

On August 3, David drove to West Virginia to complete the hiring process for the county sheriff's department. By the eleventh, David received another call informing him that they had accepted him for a position as sheriff's deputy and wanted to know when he could start.

We were utterly amazed because we did not think we would hear back from the sheriff's department in West Virginia. But now we had a decision to make—to stay where we were or take a huge step forward to begin a new career and live in a new state. After discussing it, we decided it was the right time to move forward and see what life had to offer. We had no idea where it would lead us.

Unfortunately, I only had my new job as a deputy for a month, and now I had to turn in my two weeks' notice. David had to notify the city police department, where he had worked for thirteen years, of his pending two-week resignation.

God continued to surprise us, as all the pieces came together rather quickly. Remarkably, the cut-off age to work in any field of law enforcement for the state of West Virginia was forty-five. David had just turned forty-five three months ago. This would have been his last opportunity to move to West Virginia and be hired in a job in law enforcement. Otherwise, we would have to wait until he retired so we could be closer to his family.

As we planned to live in West Virginia, we were able to buy a small two-bedroom house from David's Uncle. He had it on the market for several months and was starting to think he was not going to be able to sell it. God knew our plans to move to West Virginia and already had a place for us to live before we even thought about it.

At the same time, we had to fix up our five-bedroom house to sell. I painted bedrooms, and we hung trim and finished laying the kitchen floor. A few months prior, we had just bought new carpet for all the bedrooms and new siding for the house. We had thought about selling the house, but not this fast.

Two days before we moved completely out of our house, I had contacted a real estate agent. The day she arrived to take pictures of our house to post on their Web site, there were movers packing up all of our furniture and loading it onto a truck. I just had to shake my head and watch the giant whirlwind going on. The real estate agent even showed our house to two potential buyers on the first day it was on the market.

The next day, David and I had two separate vehicles loaded up, with our two dogs, traveling from Missouri to West Virginia. While on the road, we received a call from the real estate agent who told us we had an offer on the house. We excitedly accepted the offer, as long as they could close on the house within thirty days. This took away a major concern on how to pay two mortgages until we were able to sell the house.

The real estate agent informed us she would e-mail us the paperwork we needed to sign, and we could fax it back to her. I could not believe how quickly everything was falling into place! We did not have time to stop and think about or plan anything. We just went with the flow and knew that deep down, everything was going to work out how it should. This was the first time I had ever planned something out and I did not know the outcome. We were definitely stepping out in faith.

We arrived in West Virginia on a Friday after a ten-hour drive, and David started his new job as a deputy sheriff on Monday, August 31, 2015. His DSN (department service number) for the city police department was 831. A police officer radios into dispatch and to other officers using their DSN number.

Unfortunately, the next day, our real estate agent called us and said that the buyer's home insurance company was refusing to insure them due to the old roof that was on the house now. She informed me that the roof did appear to have hail damage and some home owner insurance will cover hail damage. Contacting our home owner insurance, we were shocked to find out that our roof was covered for hail damage and they would pay $4,000 to have the entire roof replaced.

Our real estate agent even started contacting local roofing companies for us and told us which company had the best bid. After we agreed on a company, she scheduled them, and work began right away. The real estate agent said she planned to have the roof done before the thirty days so the house closing would not be affected. Surprisingly, we were unpacking everything in our new house, and construction to our old roof was going on.

Two weeks after we moved into our new home, we were packing up and getting on a plane to get married in Maui, Hawaii. This was adding stress on top of stress, but thankfully, there was no time to stop and think. Surprisingly, we were able to relax and enjoy our honeymoon. I would never have thought of or planned on buying a house or moving out of state two weeks before getting married. I knew everything was out of my hands, but God was taking care of us.

When we returned from our honeymoon, I had to start looking for a job. I didn't really know how to pray, but I did start asking God to help me find a job. I thought maybe I could get hired at the local manufacturing company. I had heard from Uncle that the pay was really good and it was only two blocks from the house. So if I could get hired there, I would not even have to drive to work.

Within those first thirty days, a brand-new roof was placed on our old home in Missouri, and our home owner insurance covered the entire cost. Then we sold our home. This was a major stress reliever lifted off my chest. I could not believe how everything was meant to happen this way.

Approximately a month later, I got hired at Cabela's as a service desk associate. While sitting in orientation on my third day, I got a call from the human resource department at the manufacturing company located close to my home. They asked if I could come in for an interview and to bring my résumé. I could not believe it, but I knew our Uncle must have spoken to someone to get an interview scheduled. I had heard it was hard to get hired in the company unless you had family or friends who already worked for them.

The next day, I went in for an interview, and afterward they asked me to come back in the morning for a drug test. I passed the drug test, and they called me a couple of days later, asking when I wanted to started the job. Amazing! Deep down, I knew that God had answered my prayer and had ordained my footsteps. Shockingly, I discovered that the factory paid more than I made as a patrolman for the past ten years.

Recollecting the past month, I could not comprehend all the events that had transpired. David, my fiancé at the time, had passed all the West Virginia sheriff's department hiring process and got offered a position. We contacted a moving company and real estate agent to sell our home in Missouri. While we headed for our new home that we had purchased in West Virginia, we received a call from our real estate agent. She told us we had an offer on our house, and this was only the second day it was on the market.

Then David started his new job as a deputy, on Monday, two days after we arrived in West Virginia. Within that same week, we received another call from our real estate agent, saying our old roof needed to be repaired before the new home owners could purchase the house. But miraculously, the prior hail damage on the roof was paid for by our home owner insurance. This was completely unbelievable and cost us nothing.

While construction was going on at our old home, we were getting loaded onto a plane to fly to Maui, Hawaii, to be married. Aloha! Remarkably, we were able to relax and enjoy each other's company in the present moment. Even our wedding day was stress-free. We were cruising around beautiful Hawaii, taking photographs of the ocean, just hours prior to getting ready for our sunset ceremony on the beach. It was a blissful wedding and honeymoon with just the two of us.

We returned home as Mr. and Mrs. I had to continue searching for a job. At the end of the month, we sold our old home in Missouri. A couple of weeks later, I got hired in a factory and started a new occupation. Talk about a stressful month!

Just seven months prior, I had truly felt devastated, beaten down, stomped on, and as if every single door was slamming shut in my face. As I look back now, I know we were not alone through the storm. God was with us the entire time holding us up. There was no luck. It was all in God's major plan for us. Unfortunately, I still would not realize what that plan was until two years later.

All these events occurred without us having any control or knowing how everything was going to work. Honestly, it felt like every single step was already planned out for us and all we had to do was step forward in faith.

God is good, and His love never fails.

BEING SAVED

In October 2017, two years after moving to West Virginia, I found myself at a crossroads asking myself what I wanted to do with my life. Should I go back into law enforcement so I can help others? What career would I love to do?

The occupation I had now paid great wages, but it only felt like a job. I never felt like I was helping others or making a difference. In my heart, I felt that something was missing. I was unsatisfied with my job. There had to be more to life. I found myself getting extremely frustrated with work and not wanting to be there. I began questioning what my purpose in life was.

I began reading *The Purpose Driven Life* written by Rick Warren. It was an intriguing book, full of Bible scriptures, indicating how Jesus said, "I am the way, the truth, and the life. No one comes to the Father except through Me" (John 14:6). It said God wants us to receive all His promises if we follow and obey all His commandants.

I was reading the chapter where Warren mentioned how God wants us to have fellowship with the church, which is Christ's body. I recall saying to myself, "But, God, I've never been to church." I did own a Police Officer Bible but had never read it. I had no knowledge about the different chapters and verses or that there were sixty-six books in the Bible. I will admit I had a lot to learn about Jesus and God and all He had done for us.

While at work on midnight shift, I heard a faint small voice inside me mention that I needed to go to church. I remember answering, "Yeah. Yeah. I'll go." Then I pushed the idea to the back of my mind.

A week later, I was at work during the evening, and I had sent my husband several text messages. I received no response for six hours. Unfortunately, when I did not hear back from my husband while he was at work, I became very mad. Honestly, there was no reason to be frustrated or agitated. But the Devil enjoys toying with and tricking our emotions. I was receiving several terrible negative thoughts of my husband flirting with females while he was working. I tried to push those thoughts out of my mind, but then two more would take its place. It honestly felt like a battle inside me where I was being consumed by negative thoughts, cruel ideas, and emotions.

Once you allow one negative thought to enter your mind, it opens a foothold for the enemy to enter. Bad idea. Don't let this happen. For me, it allowed an ugly green jealousy monster to rise up from inside me. Suddenly, I no longer had control over my emotions. They now ruled me and my thoughts. My mind felt like it was spinning out of control with so much hate and anger. Regrettably, I was becoming more furious by the minute.

While working, I was extremely frustrated, irritated, and angry. I attempted to try to release all of my built-up frustration while using a hammer to strike the plastic material. At the same time, I had a lot of evil thoughts that continuously ran through my mind. I had reached my boiling point where I even imagined smashing the hammer down hard to hurt someone. This was when I suddenly could feel my heart tightening up and becoming hard. I then imagined a concrete wall being built by cinder blocks, stacked in front of my heart and in my mind. This feeling and image terrified me. All I knew was that I did not want to become a coldhearted, cruel, mean individual.

Then out of nowhere, I heard the small voice say, "Church!" I said to myself, "Okay, God, I hear you and I'm going."

That Sunday, October 22, 2017, I arrived at New Day Christian Church with my mother-in-law. This was the first church service I had ever attended. I was not sure what to wear or what to expect. I just knew that when God puts something on your heart, you better listen and obey.

Before the service began, my mother-in-law escorted all the kindergarten through eighth-grade kids downstairs, where she taught them Sunday school. I was left sitting upstairs, by myself, to listen to the church sermon.

It was Pastor Appreciation Day so another minister, Diane, was preaching. Diane said, "To be born again is to be saved." During her sermon, she was saying how we must surrender to God, repent all our sins. Then we must confess our sins to Him and believe that God raised Jesus from the grave. She said, "We have to empty ourselves and our hearts so Jesus and God can fill our vessel." I thought to myself, "That is exactly what I need to do." But how?

She said, "The Lord will fight our battles and you will find your peace! Be still and trust in God." Diane then said, "Get your eyes off yourself and get your eyes on God." I was amazed because those were all the words I needed to hear. I realized I needed to empty myself and stop being selfish and jealous.

After the sermon, the main pastor, Angel, said this was an altar call. She said at the end of every service she asks anyone who needs to know Jesus or wants to ask Him into their heart to come forward.

I was sitting in my seat when I heard that same small voice say, "You need to go up there." I thought to myself, "I cannot go up there. I don't know anyone in here since my mother-in-law went downstairs." The voice said, "If you don't go up there now, you won't ever do it."

I knew God was right so I collected some courage and walked up to the front of the church. I located the pastor sitting on the altar praying, and I tapped her on the shoulder. I told her, "I needed to empty myself to allow Jesus into my heart, but I did not know how to do that." She smiled at me.

Angel said all I had to do was pray this prayer out loud. Inside, I was screaming, "Oh no!" To be honest, I'm a quiet person around people I don't know. So this was a huge step for me, but I knew I had to do it.

This was the prayer I prayed out loud, "Lord, I am a sinner. Please forgive me of my sins. I believe Jesus is the Son of God, whom God raised from the grave. Jesus, please come into my heart and my life. I surrender to you, Jesus, you are my Lord and Savior. In Jesus's name. Amen."

While praying this prayer, my entire body began to tremble uncontrollably. This was the most vulnerable and raw I had ever been or felt in my life. I will admit I am not a crier and hated to even allow my husband see me cry. Here I was kneeling on the floor in front of the altar shaking like a leaf. Suddenly, it was like someone opened a floodgate full of tears.

The tears flowed freely down my face, nonstop. Surprisingly, as much as I tried to stop crying, I couldn't. As I continued to wipe away tears, I apologized to the Pastor and told her I really was not a crier. This was the first time I had ever experienced this overwhelming release of emotions.

I was amazed by the rush of emotions that washed over me. Without warning, I felt saddened by my sins then overwhelmed with so much warmth, love, and forgiveness flowing over me. There was a wave of stillness, calmness, and a peace that I have never experienced in my entire life. Unbelievably, as quickly as my tears had begun, they stopped.

Perplexed, I sat there for a moment wandering how I went from crying for the first time in public to such a peace. Just being still in Jesus's presence was an incredible feeling. I felt absolutely amazed, refreshed, rejuvenated, like a brand-new person. All I did was ask Jesus to be my Lord and Savior, to live in my heart, and forgive me for all of my sins.

I turned around to go back to my seat, and there was my mother-in-law sitting in the seat next to mine. She had so much joy and love on her face, with tears in her eyes. As I walked back to my seat, my mother-in-law gave me the warmest hug and told me, "Welcome to God's family."

Then tears swelled up in my eyes again, and we just embraced each other. For the first time, I felt completely at peace and very much loved at the same time. What a great loving family God has!

This day would always be remembered as the day God saved me! He had called me to His family, the body of Christ, the church, and adopted me as a "Child of God."

Before being born again, I was a sinner. For years, I cursed like a sailor, listened to and told crude jokes, was ruled by emotions and lusts of my flesh. When I was seventeen, I had moved out of my mom's house and lived with my first husband. I was married at nineteen, and we were divorced when I was twenty-six. But by God's grace and mercy, I was saved. It was nothing that I had done or deserved.

While growing up, it had always been my mom, my brother, and me. Today, I consciously realized I was adopted and had always had my Heavenly Father watching over me and protecting me. This was the exact moment I recognized that as a police officer, I had always been doing God's work by helping and rescuing others.

Surprisingly, every time I said the word "adopted," tears would run down my face. It just touched my heart so deeply that God loves us so much. I also now knew I was a new creation in Christ; old things have passed away, and new things have come. I no longer wanted to sin, but to obey God's commandments and follow in Jesus's footsteps.

Two days after being saved, I was still in such a state of calmness and relaxation. I had no worries, no concerns, and no anxieties. I recall sitting outside in a lawn chair watching the dogs run around in the yard, and I was completely content. I smiled to myself because I knew I had never felt this much warmth, peacefulness, and relaxation in my entire life. I wished I could bottle up this feeling to share and give to others. I never wanted it to end.

As I thanked God for His many blessings and basked in His glory, all I could do was smile.

BAPTIZED

In December 2017, almost two months after being saved and asking Jesus to come into my heart, I was baptized. To be honest, I always thought baptism was only for Catholics. I learned that the purpose of baptism is to give a visual testimony of my commitment and devotion to Christ.

We know Christ died on the cross for us so we could all be forgiven of our sins, receive eternal life, and be given the precious gift of the Holy Spirit. Jesus then rose again. Baptism symbolizes that when a person is submerged under water, they leave behind the old dead sinful life. As the person rises from the water, it resembles being cleansed with a new, fresh purposeful life.

This was the first time I was ever baptized or had witnessed one. I truthfully did not know what to expect, but I felt excited and nervous at the same time. There were two other juveniles that were getting baptized with me. All three of us had huge smiles on our faces.

Since it was winter, it was too cold to be baptized outside in the creek. Fortunately, the service was held inside a church with a heated pool. During the service, I remember having the largest grin planted on my face after surrendering my life to Jesus. I asked Him to forgive me for all of my sins and for having them washed away. I was submerged under the water, and as I rose up, I felt a huge weight had been lifted. It resembled "walking on cloud nine." It was just an amazing incredible feeling of warmth, peace, relaxation, and rejuvenation.

After we were all baptized, we received a shirt, saying, "I Have Decided to Follow Jesus"; and on the back, it said, "No Turning Back." In my heart, I knew this was my new goal in life. I was excited to see what God had planned for me next.

The Bible scripture Ephesians 4:22–24 represented my new life in Christ. It says, "You took off your former way of life the old man that is corrupted by deceitful desires; you are being renewed in the spirit of your minds; you put on the new man, the one created according to God's (likeness) in righteousness and purity of the truth."

The following month in January, the pastor made an altar call for anyone who wanted to be baptized in the Holy Spirit to come forward. I know we receive the precious gift of the Holy Spirit when we confess out loud with our mouths that Jesus is the Son of God and is our Lord and Savior. Being baptized in the Holy Spirit is just being completely filled with the Spirit, which leads to a life filled with peace, joy, free of regrets. It also enables God to use you in a supernatural way through the Spirit, which is His Spirit.

I approached the pastor and told her I wanted to be baptized in the Holy Spirit. She began praying with me and told me to just start worshipping and praising Jesus and God out loud. And for any sounds or symbols I wanted to speak, I should let them be spoken.

I knelt at the altar just worshipping and praising God and tried to tear down all the walls my mind kept putting up. Honestly, I did not think I was going receive an extra filling of the Holy Spirit and start talking in tongues. In the Bible in Acts 2:4, it says, "Then they were all filled with the Holy Spirit and began to speak in different languages, as the Spirit gave them ability for speech."

While kneeling at the altar through three songs, I felt something rising up inside me. It started out like a small wound-up ball of energy slowly moving up my leg. It was the strangest sensation I have ever experienced. Suddenly, without any warning, my right leg began violently shaking. But when I looked down, it was completely still. I had no idea what to think because I still had the sensation of my leg shaking. I then felt the vibration rise up to my stomach. Incredible! The best way I could describe this experience was like riding an old wooden roller coaster at Six Flags in St. Louis. It would rattle and shake you until the ride was over. I had never experienced any feeling like this before while just kneeling on the ground completely still.

All I could say was "Thank You. Thank You." But as I was speaking, those were not the words coming out of my mouth. I was in complete shock. The odd sounds coming out of my mouth sounded like gibberish to me. But I knew it was the Holy Spirit speaking through me, just praising God and Jesus. I was utterly amazed. I was extremely excited, and when the vibration in my leg had stopped, I was going to go back to my seat.

Suddenly, it started shaking all over again. As I spoke to say "thank you" again, those were not the words coming out of my mouth. Surprisingly, only strange knocking sounds came out. I just continued to praise and thank God for the precious gift of the Holy Spirit.

Talking in tongues is a wonderful, energizing experience and the first miracle of power to prove that Jesus is alive. The baptism of the Holy Spirit is a gift that releases God's power into and through our lives for His glory and praise. We will not understand the language we are speaking, but God understands what the Spirit is praying.

For the Bible says in Romans 8:26–27, "In the same way the Spirit also joins to help in our weakness, because we do not know what to pray for as we should, but the Spirit Himself intercedes for us with unspoken groanings. And He who searches the heart knows the Spirit's mind-set, because He intercedes for the saints according to the will of God."

First Corinthians 14:2 says, "For the person who speaks in (another) language is not speaking to men but to God."

Jesus said, "This is what you heard from Me; for John baptized with water, but you will be baptized with the Holy Spirit not many days from now" (Acts 1:5).

Then Jesus said, "But you will receive power when the Holy Spirit has come upon you, and you will be My witnesses in Jerusalem, in all Judea and Samaria, and to the ends of the earth" (Acts 1:8).

In Ephesians 6:11, Apostle Paul says, "Put on the full armor of God so that you can stand against the tactics of the Devil."

Paul then says in Ephesians 6:18, "With every prayer and request, pray at all times in the Spirit, and stay alert in this with all perseverance and intercession for all the saints."

Since I asked Jesus to be my Lord and Savior, I've had such a fire in my soul for Him and a true hunger to keep learning more. I wanted to continue getting into God's word and strengthening my relationship with Him. I had set a personal goal to read the entire Holy Bible, containing its sixty-six books within a year. Miraculously, with God's help, He had given me the confidence and desire I needed to achieve that goal. I had twenty-seven more books of the Bible to read with only a month to go, but I accomplished it.

Even today, I continue to seek God first in everything and look for ways to give, to serve, and help others. I know this is only the beginning of my walk with following the Lord, and I cannot wait to see what God has in store for me next. My journey with the Lord is just beginning.

GOD'S TIMING

God continues to prove His love for us. While we were sinners, Christ died for us. God can also get hold of anyone and change their heart of stone to flesh. But it is on His time, not ours. It took me thirty-four years to get the call to go to church, which changed my life forever. Once God calls you, you have a choice, but you have to answer.

My younger brother, Anthony, had just turned thirty-three in March of 2018. We had not spoken nor seen each other in the past two and a half years. He was someone you would describe as the total opposite of a police officer. Yep, a criminal!

As my brother was growing up, he had participated in a lot of criminal activities. Starting at the age of fifteen, he was smoking marijuana and had made a homemade tattoo gun. He even gave himself permanent tattoos, which still remain on him. Anthony also drank alcohol, did illegal drugs, and took prescription pills.

At the age of sixteen, he had been arrested several times for stealing. Anthony had tried to tell Mom that he had found the CDs in a parking lot. He just failed to mention that the CDs were taken from someone's car. I later discovered that when my brother was sixteen, he had stolen several vehicles and drove them to a "chop shop" in St. Louis. A chop shop is a business or location that disassembles stolen vehicles for the purpose of selling their parts. He had also mentioned he had tried cocaine.

Today, in his thirties, my brother was still being arrested for violating his probation. Anthony was recently arrested for driving my mother's vehicle while he was intoxicated. Unfortunately, he was still living at home in my mom's two-bedroom apartment with his girlfriend.

Back in 2015, several months before we moved to West Virginia, I received a call from my fiancé, David, asking me if my mom was home. I told him I could call her to get her exact location and asked him what was going on. He told me my brother had made a comment on Facebook, saying he was going to shoot himself with a shotgun. He asked me if my brother had any guns. I told him that I didn't know for sure.

Police officers arrived at my mom's apartment where my brother was residing and had it surrounded. Surprisingly, Anthony did open the front door, but when he saw all the police, he quickly slammed the door shut in their face. Now the officers were at a standoff with my brother locked up in the apartment. I had called my mom, and she verified she was at work and had no clue to what was going on with my brother.

The lieutenant had arrived on the scene at the apartment and told my fiancé to call my brother. Bad idea. So David called Anthony, and he answered the phone, saying, "Who the *beep* is this!" Then David lost his temper. He told him, "You know who this is. Now get out here now." Then he heard a click. The lieutenant just stared at David in disbelief of what he heard him say on the phone. Finally, the police were able to make entrance into the apartment securing my brother in handcuffs and transporting him to the hospital for evaluation.

The last time I saw Anthony was a month before we moved, at 10:00 a.m. during a weekday. He was sitting on my mom's front porch, intoxicated. I had run over to drop off an item to my mom. Anthony said in slurred words, "I'm just going to go hang myself. I have no reason to live." I was furious that he still had my mom supporting him and living in her apartment. I told him, "Go do it, and don't you dare let Mom see." Unfortunately, those were the last words I had spoken to my brother.

In August 2015, David and I moved from Missouri to West Virginia so I had no further contact with my brother. The last thing I had heard about my brother was that he had made another suicidal threat to my mom, so she had called the police. Several officers had arrived at my mom's apartment to check on my brother. They went to place Anthony in handcuffs, and he began fighting them.

I was later told by my brother that the officer was able to place a handcuff on one of his arms, but he refused to give them his other arm. He said he then used the opened handcuff to stab one of the patrolmen in his calf because he had his knee on his back. Anthony told me the officers were able to get him down, and the next thing he knew, he was waking up in the back of an ambulance, with his wrists and ankles handcuffed together. He said that at that point, he was done fighting. Anthony explained how he was transported to the hospital where he was placed on a thirty-six-hour hold for evaluation.

While at the hospital, Anthony said the officer he had stabbed with the handcuff was in the emergency room next to him. He told me that during his thirty-six-hour hold, he had to remove his eleven piercings. Anthony said that when he was about to leave after his thirty-six-hour hold, he found out he had an arrest warrant.

I was unaware of these events and could not believe this was my brother who was so rude, crude, disrespectful, inconsiderate, and ignorant to others. But growing up, I knew I wanted to become a police officer so I could arrest anyone who acted like my brother.

In March 2018, on Anthony's birthday, God put it strongly on my heart that I needed to forgive my brother. I sent my mom a text message, saying to tell my little brother happy birthday.

A couple of minutes later, I received a text message from an unknown phone number. I did not expect my mom to send a text message back because she never learned how to send texts.

It said, "Hey, sis, it's your little brother. Thanks for the birthday wishes. Love ya, be safe!" He then texted a smiley face with a halo.

I was like, "What in the world? And who is this?"

I sent a text back, saying, "Thank you," and I asked him how he had been. Anthony texted back, saying he had recently been to the police department for his job as a plumber. He said it was the first time he had gone there not in handcuffs. I was in ultimate shock.

Anthony told me that things were going well. He said he had been attending AA meetings every week and was working on getting his driver's license back. I was surprised. Then he made another statement that blew me away. My brother said he had been going to church. What! My brother! Totally unbelievable!

Hearing that Anthony was going to church for the first time in his life actually brought tears to my eyes. I felt a sudden warm sensation in my heart and was amazed how God can reach anyone. Even my unreachable brother. I know God can call anyone to Him, but it's on His timing.

I sent a text message to Anthony telling him he needed to turn his life over to Jesus and ask Him to be his Lord and Savior. And how he needed to look into getting baptized.

My brother messaged back, saying, "What have you done with my sister?" I laughed because I had forgotten that he was unaware that I had surrendered my life to Jesus.

The next text I received from Anthony surprised me even more. He said, "I believe Jesus is my Lord and Savior, but I'm not taking a bath at the church."

I just shook my head. Yea, that's my brother! But for him to claim Jesus as his Lord and Savior was earth shattering. I felt so much warmth in my heart that a tear rolled down my cheek. As I stood there, I realized God can change any heart from stone to flesh and reconcile any relationship. Especially if God could get me and my younger brother talking to each other.

I had been praying for God to soften my brother's heart, to save him, and to have him turn his life over to Jesus. God definitely answers prayers. Never stop praying!

Remember, God does answer all prayers that are within His will, but on His time. It definitely may not be as quickly as we hope, but always keep your trust in the Lord. Continue to pray and thank God every day for all your blessings and prayers answered.

New Beginning

Apostle Paul states in the Bible in Second Corinthians 5:17, "Anyone who belongs to Christ has become a new person. The old life is gone; a new life has begun!"

Within one year of being saved on October 22, 2017, I had completely changed into a new person for the better. As an officer, I would curse all the time and drop the "f-bomb" without even realizing it. Sadly, that was the only language suspects understood, and they would not respond to anyone telling them, "Please put your hands behind your back." Most patrolmen would have to speak the same disrespectful, rude, hateful language. Also working in a predominantly male environment, it was common to tell and hear crude jokes.

Unfortunately, the "old" me allowed my emotions to rule how I was feeling and how I would act to situations. This truly only leads to feeling insecure, jealous, envious, depressed, lonely, and unloved. Never a good idea. Tragically, I also had no concept of what my purpose was and felt there had to be more to life.

I also used to listen to hip-hop/rap music. This was full of foul language and lyrics degrading to women, but you could shake to the beat. But not anymore! I now only wanted to listen to Christian music. The music is uplifting, inspiring, and makes you feel closer to God.

Immediately, I realized I had to stop speaking any curse words and all foul, crude, negative language. In Psalm 34:13, it says, "Keep your tongue from evil and your lips from telling lies." James 3:9–10 says, "With the tongue we praise our Lord and Father and with it we curse human beings who have been made in God's likeness. Out of the same mouth praise and cursing. My brothers and sisters, this should not be."

I also noticed I no longer enjoyed watching television shows or movies that had crude humor, cursing, or was trying to scare me. I also started to become conscious of the clothing I wore. I caught myself not wanting to wear any of my low-cut tank tops or tee shirts. I also didn't want to wear anything that was too revealing or drawing too much attention to myself. I now only wanted to draw others' attention toward Jesus and all the blessings they could receive.

Before I became a new person in Christ, our marriage was good, but within the past year, I've noticed a drastic change for the better. I caught myself not getting angry or agitated nearly as often when my husband had to stay hours after work or had to go to work on his days off. I understood this was part of working in law enforcement and you are always on call. Even my husband mentioned he had seen a difference in my attitude.

I truly had become slow to anger and was quick to forgive. What a remarkable feeling to live in peace and to no longer be ruled by ugly, negative, bitter emotions. Plus, I was on a new walk of faith, following Jesus.

"I know the plans I have for you," declares the Lord, "plans to prosper you not to harm you, plans to give you hope and future" (Jeremiah 29:11). I am truly excited to discover all the plans God has in store for me and to better serve Him.

Unforeseen to me, looking back over my ten years in law enforcement as a patrolman, I realize that God had it all planned out. He had put the desire in my heart, at a young age, to help others by becoming a police officer. Remarkably, while working the road answering calls for service, God was with me every step of the way. He protected me and was the strength I needed to accomplish all tasks.

Without realizing it, I was doing God's work that He had called me to do. I was protecting His people, helping His injured, and giving strength to His weak. I feel truly blessed and honored that God had chosen me with a large responsibility of protecting and serving His people.

God has also chosen you and has a plan for every single one of us to carry out, whether we are aware of it at the time or not. To truly understand God's calling for your life, all you have to do is turn to Him and get into His word.

CPSIA information can be obtained
at www.ICGtesting.com
Printed in the USA
LVHW012308130519
617615LV00003B/363